Warman's
COMPANION

McCOY
POTTERY

2nd Edition

Mark F. Moran

Published by

kp **krause publications**
A subsidiary of F+W Media, Inc.

700 East State Street • Iola, WI 54990-0001
715-445-2214 • 888-457-2873
www.krausebooks.com

Our toll-free number to place an order or obtain
a free catalog is (800) 258-0929.

Library of Congress Control Number: 2008937688

ISBN-13: 978-0-89689-841-7
ISBN-10: 0-89689-841-5

Designed by Donna Mummery
Edited by Sharon Thatcher

Printed in China

On the Cover
Bottom photo: Woodsy Owl cookie jar, 1970s. Top, front: Paneled jardinière in Green Onyz
glaze, mid-1920s. Top, back: Jardinière in blended glaze, stoneware, early 1920s.

Warman's®
COMPANION

McCOY
POTTERY

2nd Edition

Mark F. Moran

Warman's® Identification and Price Guides

Warman's® American & European Art Pottery
Warman's® Antiques & Collectibles Annual Price Guide
Warman's® Carnival Glass
Warman's® Children's Books
Warman's® Civil War Collectibles
Warman's® Civil War Weapons
Warman's® Coca-Cola® Collectibles
Warman's® Coins and Paper Money
Warman's® Cookie Jars
Warman's® Costume Jewelry Figurals
Warman's® Depression Glass
Warman's® Dolls: Antique to Modern
Warman's® Duck Decoys
Warman's® English & Continental Pottery & Porcelain
Warman's® Fenton Glass
Warman's® Fiesta
Warman's® Flea Market Price Guide
Warman's® Gas Station Collectibles
Warman's® Hull Pottery

Warman's® Jewelry
Warman's® John Deere Collectibles
Warman's® Little Golden Books®
Warman's® Majolica
Warman's® McCoy Pottery
Warman's® Modernism Furniture and Accessories
Warman's® North American Indian Artifacts
Warman's® Political Collectibles
Warman's® Red Wing Pottery
Warman's® Rookwood Pottery
Warman's® Roseville Pottery
Warman's® Sporting Collectibles
Warman's® Sterling Silver Flatware
Warman's® Vietnam War Collectibles
Warman's® Vintage Jewelry
Warman's® Vintage Quilts
Warman's® Weller Pottery
Warman's® World War II Collectibles

Warman's® Companions

Carnival Glass Warman's® Companion
Collectible Dolls Warman's® Companion
Collectible Fishing Lures Warman's® Companion
Depression Glass Warman's® Companion
Fenton Glass Warman's® Companion
Fiesta Warman's® Companion
Hallmark Keepsake Ornaments Warman's® Companion
Hot Wheels Warman's® Companion

McCoy Pottery Warman's® Companion
PEZ® Warman's® Companion
Roseville Pottery Warman's® Companion
U.S. Coins & Currency Warman's® Companion
Watches Warman's® Companion
World Coins & Currency Warman's® Companion

Warman's® Field Guides

Warman's® Action Figures Field Guide
Warman's® Antique Jewelry Field Guide
Warman's® Barbie Doll Field Guide
Warman's® Bean Plush Field Guide
Warman's® Bottles Field Guide
Warman's® Buttons Field Guide
Warman's® Coca-Cola® Field Guide
Warman's® Depression Glass Field Guide
Warman's® Disney Collectibles Field Guide
Warman's® Dolls Field Guide
Warman's® Farm Toys Field Guide
Warman's® Field Guide to Precious Moments®
Warman's® Fishing Lures Field Guide
Warman's® G.I. Joe Field Guide
Warman's® Hot Wheels Field Guide
Warman's® Kitschy Kitchen Collectibles Field Guide

Warman's® Lionel Train Field Guide 1945-1969
Warman's® Lunch Boxes Field Guide
Warman's® Matchbox Field Guide
Warman's® Pepsi Field Guide
Warman's® Star Wars Field Guide
Warman's® Tools Field Guide
Warman's® Transformers Field Guide
Warman's® U.S. Coins & Currency Field Guide
Warman's® U.S. Stamps Field Guide
Warman's® Vintage Guitars Field Guide
Warman's® Watches Field Guide
Warman's® Zippo Lighters Field Guide

Contents

Introduction
State of the Market Report

Part of the charm in collecting McCoy pottery is that, while rare pieces do command big prices, collectors can find countless pieces that won't break the bank. That, combined with over 16 decades of family pottery-making history, makes it hugely popular.

"The pottery produced some of everything, and this may be one of the appealing features of the pottery," notes Dewayne Imsand, Vice President of the McCoy Pottery Collectors' Society (mccoypotterycollectorssociety.org) and editor of the Society's quarterly *Journal*.

Yet, like many things, the market for McCoy has changed with the popularity of eBay. Over 1500 McCoy pieces are offered daily on the auction website (typically the most listings for any pottery), resulting in a major decline in prices for lower to medium priced pieces. Meanwhile, prices for the upper one-third has softened slightly, while the top 5-10% have held their values.

"There does not seem to be an especially 'hot' pottery line or era," observes Imsand. "But rather what is 'hot' is the 'cream of the crop' type pieces. When one of these type pieces show up for sale in the public market, the interest is very intense."

McCoy Limited products from the 1980s have grown the most in popularity in recent years, Imsand goes on to explain. Still, pieces from the 1930s through the early 1960s retain the largest interest overall. The earlier pieces have a form that is a bit more 'art pottery' as opposed to the volume vase and planter production of the '40s and '50s. Specific collecting areas with a high interest currently are: flower forms, miniature pieces, pastel pieces from the early 1940s, animal shaped pieces, and wall pockets.

Imsand stresses the importance of good reference books and collector clubs when pursuing McCoy Pottery. "As with most things, knowledge is very important, so get a good reference book with a reputation for accuracy of information," he says. "Also, email experienced collectors with your questions and read the articles they have written."

Fakes and reproductions continue to flourish and confuse. "The novice collector is the most vulnerable to this fraudulent activity," Imsand cautions, adding, "Knowledge is the key to combating this collector threat. Most serious collectors, with a few years of collecting experience, become aware of methods to avoid these undesirable pieces, and the sellers of them."

Collector clubs continue to provide valuable resources for their members. The McCoy Pottery Collectors' Society itself publishes a quarterly journal with tips and information.

Imsand also recommends attending special pottery events such as the annual July Pottery Festival in Zanesville, Ohio. In this way, collectors can interact with other collectors and gain a wealth of knowledge.

Despite the ups and downs of collecting, most collectors thrive on the thrill of discovery. "That is one of the great aspects about collecting McCoy pottery," Imsand says. "Not a year goes by that some undiscovered piece that was not produced surfaces for all to admire and enjoy. In addition, test pieces, or pieces with an odd glaze coloring, or a personally decorated piece by an employee for their own use, continues to regularly surface."

A case in point was the recent discovery of a large quantity of sketches done in pencil by the talented McCoy designer Leslie Cope. The sketches are of pieces produced in the 1940s and '50s by McCoy along with pieces that were never produced. The drawings were discovered by family member Velma Cope. Some of them were framed and sold to collectors.

If you are thinking about starting a McCoy collection, Imsand says to buy chosen pieces regularly. "The larger the display, the better your McCoy will look," he says. "Over time most collectors with some experience have figured that out, which is why we are known as volume collectors. However, do not be afraid to buy an expensive piece on occasion. It will most probably be the best investment of all, and it will greatly enhance your collection."

USING THE GUIDE…

This book does not contain every single piece of McCoy pottery. No book does, and perhaps no single book could. The variety and volume of wares produced by the various McCoy potteries are staggering. Also be aware that market conditions can fluctuate; thus, the prices offered here should only be used as a guide.

A Family Tradition

The first McCoy with clay under his fingernails was W. Nelson McCoy. With his uncle, W.F. McCoy, he founded a pottery works in Putnam, Ohio, in 1848, making stoneware crocks and jugs.

That same year, W. Nelson's son, James W., was born in Zanesville, Ohio. James established the J.W. McCoy Pottery Co. in Roseville, Ohio, in the fall of 1899. The J.W. McCoy plant was destroyed by fire in 1903, and was rebuilt two years later.

It was at this time that the first examples of Loy-Nel-Art wares were produced. The line's distinctive title came from the names of James McCoy's three sons, Lloyd, Nelson, and Arthur. Like other "standard" glazed pieces produced at this time by several Ohio potteries, Loy-Nel-Art has a glossy finish on a dark brown-black body, but Loy-Nel-Art featured a splash of green color on the front, and a burnt-orange splash on the back.

George Brush became general manager of J.W. McCoy Pottery Co. in 1909. The company became Brush-McCoy Pottery Co. in 1911, and in 1925 the name was shortened to Brush Pottery Co. This firm remained in business until 1982.

Separately, in 1910, Nelson McCoy Sr. founded the Nelson McCoy Sanitary and Stoneware Co., also in Roseville. By the early 1930s, production had shifted from utilitarian wares to art pottery, and the company name was changed to Nelson McCoy Pottery.

Designer Sydney Cope was hired in 1934, and was joined by his son, Leslie, in 1936. The Copes' influence on McCoy wares continued until Sydney's death in 1966. That same year, Leslie opened a gallery devoted to his family's design heritage and featuring his own original art.

Nelson McCoy Sr. died in 1945, and was succeeded as company president by his nephew, Nelson McCoy Melick.

A fire destroyed the plant in 1950, but company officials—including Nelson McCoy Jr., then 29—decided to rebuild, and the new Nelson McCoy Pottery Co. was up and running in just six months.

Nelson Melick died in 1954. Nelson Jr. became company president, and oversaw the company's continued growth. In 1967, the operation was sold to entrepreneur David Chase. At this time, the words

A fire destroyed the McCoy factory in 1950, but the plant was rebuilt and was operating again in six months.

Workers inspect the burned-out remains of the McCoy pottery factory in 1950.

"Mt. Clemens Pottery" were added to the company marks. In 1974, Chase sold the company to Lancaster Colony Corp., and the company marks included a stylized "LCC" logo. Nelson Jr. and his wife, Billie, who had served as a products supervisor, left the company in 1981.

In 1985, the company was sold again, this time to Designer Accents. The McCoy pottery factory closed in 1990.

Company Marks

USA

Early 1940s

Early 1940s-1960s

FLORALINE

Early-mid 1940s
Made for the florist trade

Late 1960
Mt. Clemens

USA

Early 1940s

U S A

1939-1960s

Late 1920s-on
Stoneware

Early-mid 1940s

Made in USA

1940s-1960s

1940s-late 1960s

Late 1940s

Late 1920s-on
Stoneware

Early 1940-1960s

Cook and Serve line

1970s
Lancaster Colony

Fakes and Reproductions of McCoy Pottery

By Mark Chervenka

Reproductions and fakes of cookie jars, vases, wall pockets, bookends, pitchers and other shapes marked "McCoy" have been increasingly common in recent years. New pieces are particularly common in online auctions. Copies of various McCoy marks have been used on the fakes. The most common is the raised molded "McCoy" mark but variations, including early marks, are also used. "USA" may or may not be included in the new marks.

A reproduction Bird and Cherries pattern 4-3/4" pitcher. This new piece is available for **$10 in pink, blue, yellow and green, shown here**. Only the new pitcher is marked. The original pitcher was never marked. Any marked piece is new.

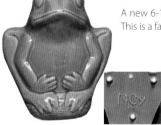

A new 6-1/2" figural frog wall vase marked "McCoy USA." This is a fantasy piece; there is no old McCoy counterpart.

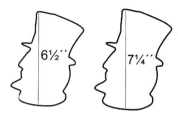

This is the new Uncle Sam vase marked McCoy. Originals were made in only three colors: aqua, yellow and white. New pieces are sold in aqua, yellow, white, pink, blue and green. The authentic Uncle Sam vase is 7-1/4" high; the reproductions are 6-1/2" high.

Both new and old Uncle Sam vases are marked "McCoy" in the base. Marks on new and old are virtually identical and are not a reliable test of age.

themselves on the latest reproductions and how they differ from the originals.

One of the best ways to detect reproductions of original McCoy shapes is size. In the process of making a new mold from an original figure, the resulting reproduction is substantially smaller than the original. Simply measuring a suspected piece is one of the best tests of unmasking a reproduction.

The reproduction Uncle Sam vase, for example, is only 6-1/2 inches tall; the original is 7-1/4 inches, a very noticeable 3/4-inch difference. Similarly, the many new cookie jars are likewise one-half to almost one-inch smaller than the originals. Size is especially important if you choose to buy without a hands-on inspection such as an online auction. Be sure to request the seller provide exact measurements. Many Internet sellers as

Fake McCoy marks are appearing not only on reproductions of shapes originally made by McCoy, but also on pieces originally made by other potteries such as Shawnee, Hull and unknown makers. This situation makes it difficult for buyers, particularly new collectors who often rely on marks to date and authenticate items. Marks alone are not a reliable test of age. Buyers now need to regularly update

A new frog sprinkler marked "McCoy." The frog is a direct copy of a vintage original. The original frog was made as a planter only, never as a sprinkler. Any piece with a handle is a fake.

well as live-auction advertisements frequently round measurements in descriptions. The 6-1/2 inch Uncle Sam vase could easily be listed as 7 inches. And don't let sellers tell you that "sizes vary" among originals. Originals were carefully manufactured under strict quality control. Very slight size variations of 1/16-inch are normal, but 1/8-inch or more is highly suspicious.

Next to size, color is probably the next best test to catch McCoy copies. Many new pieces are made in colors never used in original production. The authentic standard McCoy mailbox, for example, was made only in green. New mailboxes are made in five colors. The great majority of original Lady In Bonnet wall vases are white. Reproductions are sold in cobalt blue, green, pink and white. Any color other than white is automatically worth a closer look.

Any manufacturing details, such as glaze and paint, are generally more reliable clues to age than marks alone. Most, but not all, painted trim on vintage McCoy, for example, was applied over the glaze in unfired, or cold, paint. Many reproductions, especially the new cookie jars, have trim applied under the glaze. Many new pieces have an exaggerated crazing in the glaze deliberately created at the factory to suggest "age" and use. Dark brown or black craze lines, widely separated line of crazing and craz-

A fantasy 4-1/2" elephant bank with "GOP" molded on the side. The base is marked "McCoy." There is no original vintage McCoy counterpart to this piece.

ing over the entire surface are all warning signs of a reproduction. Although it's not unusual to find crazing on vintage McCoy, crazing on original examples is rarely over the entire surface, the lines are finer and closer together and not uniformly dark as crazing on reproductions and fakes.

The clay is also different. The great majority of original McCoy pottery was made of Ohio-based clays fired at high temperatures. It is fairly heavy and has a slight yellow to brown cast. Almost all the reproductions are made of modern white ceramic compounds typically found in china painting classes and designed for relatively low temperature firings. It is almost pure white with no color cast.

When considering a purchase, force yourself to get in the habit of confirming the original maker of any piece you see marked McCoy. Any piece offered as vintage McCoy should logically be listed in at least one or more of the many fine McCoy reference books. If you can't locate the piece in a reference book, be extremely wary.

The most common reason the vast majority of pieces marked McCoy can't be found in McCoy books is because they were originally made by another company, not McCoy. Any Little Red Riding Hood cookie jar marked McCoy is obviously a fake. The original Red Riding Hood jars were made by Hull Pottery, not McCoy. Other original Hull shapes and patterns, such as the wall pocket and cornucopia in Royal Woodland, have also been reproduced with McCoy marks. Again, any piece in Royal Woodland is automatically a fake; no measuring or other checks are needed. Similarly, pieces originally made by Shawnee and other recognized vintage potteries also appear with McCoy marks. Obviously, products known to be made by other potteries should not be marked McCoy.

Perhaps the most confusing pieces marked McCoy are those copied from vintage pieces made by other manufacturers. Examples of such items include a wall pocket of a cat with a ball of yarn, a figural elephant bank marked "GOP" and a figural frog wall pocket. All of the subjects of those pieces—frogs, kittens, banks and elephants—enjoy wide interest. While many McCoy collectors realize those items are not vintage McCoy pieces, many cat, frog, wall pocket, elephant and bank collectors do not. Seeing the McCoy mark, they incorrectly assume the pieces can't possibly be of recent manufacture.

Many of these fantasy items are often sold as "experimental pieces," "rare and unlisted items" or "after hours work." That's why, unethical sellers explain, the pieces can't be found in reference books. Don't fall for such stories and similar nonsense. The most likely reason a piece can't be found in a reference book is because it's a fake.

The original Uncle Sam vase was made during the 1940s. Both new and old are marked McCoy

A fake Little Red Riding Hood wall vase/planter marked "McCoy." This piece is a direct copy of a vintage original sold by Hull Pottery, not McCoy. Any piece marked McCoy is automatically a fake.

on the base. General production originals were made in only three colors: pale green (aqua), yellow and white. At least four different colors have been produced in the new vase including aqua, green, pink, blue, white and yellow. Some original vases and some new vases have cold-painted decorations. Most original Uncle Sam vases sell for $40 to $50. The new Uncle Sam vases sell wholesale for $12 each.

The best test of age is to measure the piece. Original Uncle Sam vases are 7-1/4 inches tall; new pieces are 6-1/2 inches tall.

Both new and old are marked McCoy in the base; marks on new and old are virtually identical and not a reliable test of age.

Original McCoy turtle flower holders were produced during the 1940s. The great majority of originals were matte glaze. So far, all the new turtles have a shiny glaze. Both new and old turtles are marked "NM, USA" molded on the side. Original turtles are known in white, blue and pale green, which are the most common; yellow and rose, which are harder to find; and brown, which is rare. New turtles have been available in a variety of colors including a cobalt blue never originally made. Bases on both new and old turtles are unglazed. New turtles are slightly smaller measuring 1-3/4 inches at the highest point. Originals are 2 inches at the same point.

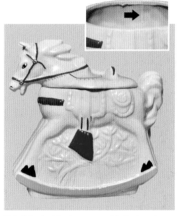

This fake hobby horse cookie jar has been made in China since the late 1990s. The original was introduced in 1948 and was available in white or decorated with an under glaze brown and green. Originals are 10-1/4" high and marked "McCoy" on the base. The reproduction hobby horses are not marked McCoy and the quality is very poor. Outsides of new jars are trimmed in brightly colored paint. There are numerous obvious paint drips throughout the jar, inside and out.

Mark Chervenka is the publisher of the Internet-based *Antiques and Collectors Reproduction News* (www.repronews.com) and America's most recognized expert on antique fakes and reproductions. He's authored four editions of *Antique Trader Guide to Fakes & Reproductions*, as well as *Antique Trader Fakes & Forged Marks*.

WARES MADE BY
J.W. MCCOY POTTERY CO.

J.W. McCoy miniature jardinière in a Carnelian glaze, circa 1903, marked 3, 3" h, **$50+**.

J.W. McCoy miniature jardinière in a blue blended glaze, circa 1903, marked 3, 3" h, **$50+**.

J.W. McCoy jardinière in a blended glaze, 1903-4, style #821, 7-3/4" h, 11" diameter, **$250+**.

J.W. McCoy miniature jardinière and pedestal, blended glaze, 1903, unmarked, overall 12" h, **$150+** set.

J.W. McCoy jardinière in a Carnelian glaze, style #93, circa 1905, marked 93, 8" h, 10" diameter, **$125+**.

J.W. McCoy jardinière in a blended glaze, style #83, circa 1905, marked 83, 8" h, 11" diameter, **$125+**.

J.W. McCoy jardinière in a Carnelian glaze, style #56, circa 1905, unmarked, 8-1/2" h, 9-1/2" diameter, **$100+**.

J.W. McCoy miniature jardinière and pedestal in a blended glaze, circa 1910, unmarked, overall 8-3/4" h, **$125+**.

J.W. McCoy jardinière and pedestal in a Carnelian glaze, circa 1905, unmarked, overall 20-1/2" h, **$400+**.

J.W. McCoy pedestal in the Olympia glaze, style #53, circa 1904, 19" h, **$250+**.

J.W. McCoy pedestal in a blended cobalt glaze, style #53, circa 1904, 19" h, **$250+**.

J.W. McCoy pedestal in the Wavy Tulip pattern, matte green glaze, 1915, unmarked, 16-1/2" h, **$200+**.

J.W. McCoy mug in a Carnelian glaze, 1904, marked N 12, 4" h, **$75+**.

J.W. McCoy jardinière in a Carnelian glaze, style #9, circa 1905, unmarked, 9-1/2" h, 10-1/2" diameter, **$125+**.

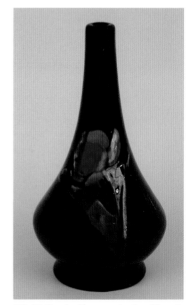

J.W. McCoy bottle vase in the Olympia glaze, circa 1905, impressed with a conjoined MC and Olympia in script, 8-3/4" h, **$125+**.

J.W. McCoy three-handled mug or tyg, circa 1905, unmarked, 8-1/4" h, **$250+**.

J.W. McCoy mug, Carnelian glaze, gilt sponge work on handle and rim, early 1900s, unmarked, 5-3/4" h, **$150-$175**.

J.W. McCoy mug, Carnelian glaze, gilt sponge work on handle and rim, early 1900s, unmarked, 5-3/4" h, **$150-$175**.

J.W. McCoy pitcher in a Carnelian glaze, 1904-5, marked 8, 8" h, **$125+**.

J.W. McCoy beer maiden pitcher in a blended glaze, circa 1915, style #34, unmarked, rare, 11" h, **$500-$600**.

J.W. McCoy beer maiden pitcher in the Olympia glaze, circa 1915, style #34, 11" h, unmarked, rare, **$550-$650**.

J.W. McCoy bud vase in a blended glaze, circa 1905, marked 4.0, 4-1/4" h, **$90+**.

J.W. McCoy umbrella stand in the Wavy Tulip pattern, matte green glaze, circa 1915, unmarked, 20-3/4" h, **$600-$700**.

From left: J.W. McCoy ewer vase in Carnelian glaze; Rosewood grapes vase, early 1900s, both unmarked; ewer, 7-1/2" h, **$200-$225;** vase, 6-1/2" h, **$190-$250**.

J.W. McCoy vases in Carnelian glaze, early 1900s, marked 10, 8-1/4" h, **$200-$225;** 6-1/2" h, **$125-$150**.

J.W. McCoy Parrot wall pocket in Peach Ivo-Tint glaze, circa 1915, unmarked, 6" h, **$150+**.

J.W. McCoy Olympia vase, with rare cream-drip glaze overflow, early 1900s, marked 28, 5-1/4" h, **$195-$225**.

J.W. McCoy squat vase in a blended glaze, circa 1905, unmarked, 6" h, **$150+**.

J.W. McCoy Olympia jug vase with a corn motif, 1905, marked with conjoined MC and Olympia in script, 7-1/2" h, **$150-$200**.

J.W. McCoy bud vase in the Olympia glaze, circa 1905, unmarked, 8-3/4" h, **$125-$150**.

J.W. McCoy Rosewood flared vase, circa 1910, unmarked, 6-1/4" h, **$125+**.

WARES MADE BY BRUSH-MCCOY POTTERY CO.

Brush-McCoy clock and candlestick set in a Green Onyx glaze, mid-1920s, unmarked; candlesticks, 6" h; clock, 4-1/2" h, **$150-$200** set.

Brush-McCoy candle holders in a Brown Onyx glaze, 1920s, marked 033, **$125+** pair.

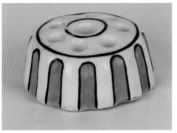

Brush-McCoy flower frog in the Lotus pattern, 1917, unmarked, 2-3/4" diameter, **$20+**.

Brush-McCoy flower bowl and frog in an Amaryllis glaze, 1920s; bowl, 6-1/4" diameter; frog, 2-1/4" h, unmarked, **$125+** pair.

Brush-McCoy bowl and flower frog (this frog is known as the mushroom with turtle sunning itself) in an early Brown Onyx glaze, 1920s; frog, 4" diameter, **$75+**; bowl, 8-3/4" diameter, unmarked, **$25**.

Brush-McCoy flower bowl and frog in Colonial Blue matte, circa 1925; bowl, 6-1/2" diameter; frog, 2-3/4" h, **$200+** set.

Brush-McCoy flower bowl and frog in the Amaryllis pattern, Ivo-Tint glaze, circa 1925; bowl (style 01), 7-1/4" diameter; frog, 2-3/4" h, **$125+** set.

Brush-McCoy jardinière, style #274, circa 1915, marked 274, 6" h, 7" diameter, **$50+**.

Three pieces of Brush-McCoy "Avenue of Trees" (also called "Woodland"), circa 1918; larger flowerpot, style #233, 5-1/2" h, **$75+**; smaller flowerpot, style #233, 4" h, **$50+**; sprouting bowl, **$30+**.

Brush-McCoy flower bowl and frog in a brown matte glaze, circa 1925; faceted bowl, 8-1/2" diameter; frog, 2-3/4" h, unmarked, **$200+**.

Brush-McCoy jardinière in the Vogue pattern, circa 1916, ink stamped "Vogue – Brush-McCoy P. Co. – Zanesville, O.," 7-1/4" h, 9" diameter, **$125+**.

Brush-McCoy jardinière in the Vogue pattern, circa 1916, ink stamped, 10-1/2" h, 11" diameter opening, **$250+**. This is the largest size.

Brush-McCoy jardinière and pedestal in a majolica glaze, Irises with Pointy Leaves, style #2340, 1913-15; jardinière, 10" h, 11-1/2" diameter; pedestal, 17" h, unmarked, **$450+** set.

Brush-McCoy jardinière and pedestal in a majolica glaze, Irises with Pointy Leaves, style #2340, 1913-15; jardinière, 12" h, 14" diameter; pedestal, 21" h, unmarked, **$550+** set.

Brush-McCoy jardinière in a blended glaze, style #234, circa 1917, marked 234, 6-1/2" h, 8" diameter, **$60+**.

Brush-McCoy jardinière in the Wavy Tulip pattern, majolica glaze, circa 1919, unmarked, 10" h, 11" diameter, **$200+**.

Brush-McCoy "Avenue of Trees" (also called "Woodland") jardinière and pedestal, style #2150, circa 1920; jardinière, 11" h, 12" diameter; pedestal, 17-1/2" h, **$550+** set.

Brush-McCoy jardinière and pedestal in the Greek Key pattern, style #116, early 1920s; jardinière, 10-1/2" h, 12" diameter; pedestal, 23-1/2" h, unmarked, **$500+** set.

Two Brush-McCoy pedestals in blended glazes, style #234, circa 1918, unmarked, 10-1/2" h, **$70+** each.

Two Brush-McCoy pedestals in blended drip glazes, stoneware, 1920s, unmarked, 12-1/2" h, **$75+** each.

Brush-McCoy jardinière and pedestal in the Lotus pattern, 1917, unmarked, 17-1/2" and 9-1/2" h, **$700+** set.

Brush-McCoy pedestal in the Easter Lily pattern, blended glaze, 1920s, unmarked, 16" h, **$150+**.

Three Brush-McCoy miniature pedestals in blended glazes, circa 1915-20, bottom two style #234, 8" h; top style #117-0, 7" h, **$50+** each.

Brush-McCoy "Avenue of Trees" (also called "Woodland") pitcher, circa 1918, marked 131, 7" h, **$100+**.

Brush-McCoy pedestal in the Easter Lily pattern, blended glaze, 1920s, unmarked, 16" h, **$150+**.

Brush-McCoy pitcher in a Blue Onyx glaze, 1920s, unmarked, 7-1/4" h, **$75+**.

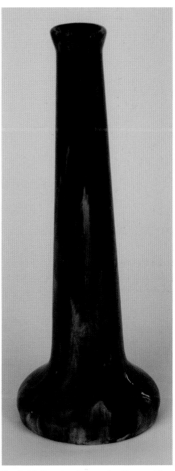

Brush-McCoy hanging planter in the Vogue pattern, with original chain, circa 1916, unmarked, 6-1/4" h, 8" diameter, **$250+**.

Brush-McCoy bud vase in Brown Onyx glaze, 1920s, marked 047, 10-1/4" h, **$50+**.

Brush-McCoy umbrella stand in a blended glaze, with Liberty Bell and Independence Hall, circa 1915, marked 73 and 4 in a circle, 22-1/2" h, **$500+**.

Brush-McCoy bud vase in a Blue Onyx glaze, 1920s, unmarked, 3" h, **$30-$40**.

Brush-McCoy vase in Green Onyx glaze, 1920s, marked 047, 10" h, **$85+**.

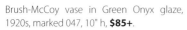

Brush-McCoy bottle vase in early Brown Onyx glaze, 1920s, 10-1/2" h, **$100+**.

Brush-McCoy vase in an early Blue Onyx glaze, early 1920s, unmarked, 5" h, **$50+**.

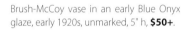

Brush-McCoy flared vase in Green Onyx glaze, 1920s, marked 10, 7-1/4" h, **$60+**.

Cookie Jars

Cookie jars represent one of most popular categories for McCoy collectors. Even the most enthusiastic collectors admit that the McCoy lid designs and configurations contribute to the dings and cracks common on these pieces, so condition is an important consideration. Many jars also have cold-paint decoration (done by hand on top of the glazed surfaces) and this paint is easily worn. Examples with good paint bring a premium price.

This category has also been plagued by fakes. Knowing the correct dimensions of the real jars is vital for beginning collectors.

Cookie jars are listed alphabetically by name/subject matter.

Apollo jar with original paper flag and label, 1970-71, McCoy mark, **$350-$400**.

Two Apple jars. Red example is late 1950s, McCoy USA mark, and same form as Blushing Apple jars, but is cold-painted with gold finial, **$75-$85**. White Apple jar, nicknamed "The Tooth," has a leaf lid found on other fruit-form jars, early 1970s, McCoy USA mark, **$50-$60**.

Two variations of Apple jars: left, as it came from the factory without leaf knob; right, flat-leaf apple with strong burgundy and yellow glaze.

Asparagus jar, 1970s, **$75-$85**.

Astronaut jar, 1960s, USA mark, **$350-$400;** this is rarely found in dark blue.

Hand-painted ball jar with slanted knob (also comes with rectangular knob), stoneware, late 1930s to early 1950s, unmarked, **$45-$55,** depending on paint condition. This shape was reissued in the mid-1960s.

Ball jar in cobalt blue, 1940s, unmarked, 6-1/2" h, **$90-$110**.

Two versions of the Banana jar, 1948, McCoy mark. Left is the more typical glaze, **$200-$250,** depending on color. This is often found with damage to lid points.

Baseball Boy and Football Boy jars, late 1970s to early '80s, McCoy USA mark, **$175-$225** each, with the Baseball Boy in the higher range. Beware of reproductions.

Barn jar with cow in door, 1960s, McCoy USA mark, lid was easily damaged, **$350-$400**.

Two Basket-weave jars, late 1950s, McCoy USA mark, one topped with apples, the other with pears. The word "Cookies" was cold-painted and is often worn; often found with damage to fruit, **$100-$125** each.

Two Basket-weave jars, late 1950s, McCoy USA mark, one topped with pine cones, the other with a puppy. The word "Cookies" was cold-painted and is often worn; often found with damage to lids, **$100-$125** each.

Two versions of the Bear with Cookie in Vest. At left is an unusual color combination with cold-painted lid, **$350-$450**. At right, jar has cold-paint trim on white, **$90-$110**. Originally from the mid-1940s, this jar was also made in the 1950s with the word "Cookies" between the bear's feet.

Reproduction Bear with Cookie in Vest, left, next to the original. The new jar is shorter and much lighter than the original and was not made by McCoy, despite having an impressed McCoy mark on the base.

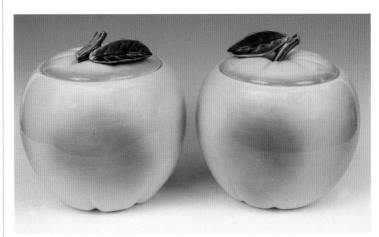

Two Blushing Apple jars, 1950s and '60s, McCoy USA mark. The example at left has the leaf finial in the wrong position. Typically about **$75**; with misplaced finial, **$100**. This is rarely found with saw-tooth leaf on lid.

Left: Bobby Baker jar, 1970s, McCoy USA mark, also comes in lower flat hat, **$50-$60**. Right: Betsy Baker, 1970s, McCoy USA mark, also comes in ruffled hat, **$175-$225**. With rare rounded hat with button top, called "Betty Baker." No established value.

Clockwise from top left: Bubbles the Pig jar/bank with original box, late 1970s; Chilly Willy in factory glazes with original box, McCoy USA mark; Teddy and Friend in factory glazes with original box; **$75-$100 each**.

Left: reproduction Cauliflower Mammy jar, **$25-$30**. Right: real Cauliflower Mammy jar with expected worn cold paint, **$500-$600**. Prices for this jar once hovered around $1,000, but the reproductions have driven values down.

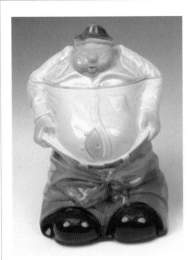

Chairman of the Board (comes in either maroon pants or brown pants), 1985, marked 162-USA, **$400-$500**.

Chilly Willy holiday variation, hand-painted at home in Christmas colors by a McCoy employee, late 1980s, USA mark; because of paint, **$175-$225;** normally, **$75-$100**.

Chef, 1960s, McCoy USA mark, **$175-$200**. This is also found with a blue face and other scarf colors. Beware of reproductions shorter than 11".

Chipmunk jar, early 1960s, McCoy USA mark, **$100-$125**. This is easily distinguished from the rare and expensive Squirrel jar—sometimes called Fox Squirrel—which has a much larger tail and is valued at about **$4,000**.

Left: Stagecoach jar, also comes in white with gold trim, hard to find, and paint wear affects value only slightly, **$700-$800**. Right: Circus Horse with Monkey jar, 1961, McCoy USA mark, cold-painted details, easily damaged, **$150-$200**.

Two versions of Clown in a Barrel, mid-1950s, McCoy USA mark, cold-painted details on all white example, all green example is rare, **$400-$500** each.

Two versions of Clown in a Barrel jar, mid-1950s, McCoy USA mark, cold-painted details, **$100-$125**.

Cookie Box (also called the Jewel Box), 1963, USA mark, **$150-$175**.

Clyde the Dog jar, mid-1970s, McCoy USA LCC mark, cold-painted details, **$250-$300**.

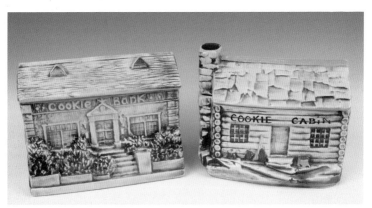

From left: Cookie Bank (model of the actual Main Street bank building in Roseville, Ohio), with money slot on reverse, 1960s, McCoy Bank mark; Cookie Cabin, 1950s, unmarked, with cold-painted details, **$90-$110** each.

Cookie Boy jar in turquoise with crisp mold detail, early 1940s, McCoy mark, **$300-$350**. Rarely found bare headed.

Cookie Boy jars in yellow and white, early 1940s, McCoy mark, **$200-$225** each.

Two cookie jars in gold trim, late 1940s to '50s. Sack of Cookies has McCoy USA mark, other jar unmarked, **$40-$50** each.

Cookie Special jar, early 1960s, McCoy USA mark, cold-painted details, **$125-$175**.

From left: Cookie Wagon (also called the "Conestoga Wagon"), 1960s, McCoy USA mark, with glaze and cold paint, **$75-$90**. Cookie House, late 1950s, McCoy USA mark, with split roof lid, easily damaged, with glaze and cold paint, **$125-$140**.

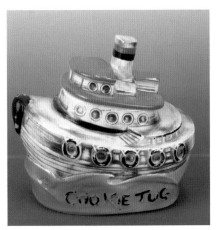

Cookie Tug jar with cold-paint decoration, 1950s, McCoy USA mark, **$8,000-$10,000**.

Cork crock jar, 1975, McCoy USA mark, can be hard to find complete because lid often broke, **$90-$110**.

Dalmatians in Rocking Chair, early 1960s, McCoy USA Dalmatians mark, **$325-$375**. Beware of reproductions shorter than 9".

Down on the Farm Cow, early 1990s, Designer Accents mark, **$90-$110**. This is not to be confused with the rare Reclining Cow—also known as "Cookies and Milk Cow"—which sold at auction for **$10,000**.

Left: reproduction Davy Crockett jar; right: original Crockett jar, late 1950s, USA mark, all decoration under glaze, **$450-$550**. Prices for this jar once hovered around **$700**, but the reproductions have driven values down.

Two versions of Doghouse with Bird jar; the one at left is more common, 1980s, later reissued by Lancaster Colony, **$175-$200**. The same dog and bird forms on the front of the jar were found on a rare pair of bookends—possibly for sales samples— that sold at auction for **$4,000**.

Two versions of the Drum jar, 1960, McCoy USA mark, all cold-painted so examples may be found nearly white. Red, white, and blue is more common than brown and yellow, **$90-$110** each.

Duck on Basket-weave, 1950s, McCoy USA mark, cold-painted details, **$90-$110**.

Dutchman cookie jar with cold-paint decoration, 1945, McCoy mark, 9-1/2" h, **$55-$70**.

Engine jar, early 1960s, McCoy USA mark, cold-painted details, **$125-$175**, with other color combinations found on engine.

Two other color combinations for Engine jar, **$250-$300** each.

Two versions of the Elephant jar, both with cold-painted details. Example at left is called "split trunk" and is harder to find, 1940s, unmarked, **$275-$300**. Example at right has complete trunk as part of lid, 1950s, unmarked, **$150-$175**.

Fireplace lamp and cookie jar made from the same mold, late 1960s, USA mark, **$75-$100** for the jar; **$125-$150** for the lamp (rare).

Forbidden Fruit jar, late 1960s, McCoy USA mark, with cold paint on the lid, **$90-$110**.

Flat-leaf Apple cookie jar, glossy maroon, 1930s, **$125-$150**.

Flowerpot jar, 1960s, flower forms vary and can be replaced, **$175-$225**.

Freddie the Gleep, mid-1970s, cold-paint details (also available in lime green), has been reproduced slightly smaller, **$350-$400**.

Friendship 7 jar, 1960s, unmarked, cold-paint details, **$100-$125**.

Globe jar, cold-painted details, 1960, McCoy USA mark, **$250-$300**.

Happy Face cookie jar, 1970s McCoy LCC mark, 11" h, **$65-$85**.

Hamm's Bear jar, early 1970s, USA mark, also found with white tie, **$225-$250**.

Granny with Glasses jar: on the left is the model used to make molds, and the production jar is at right, 1970s, USA mark, **$90-$110**. Also found in white with gold trim.

Grapes jar with bird on lid in air-brushed colors, non-production piece, McCoy mark, 9-1/2" h, **$7,000+**.

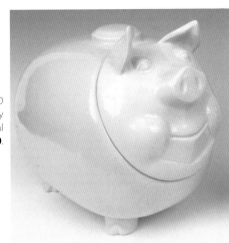

Harley Hog bank, 1984, HD McCoy mark but not made by McCoy, also found with decal and contrasting cap, **$90-$110**.

Hobnail jars, stoneware, in yellow and hard-to-find cobalt, early 1940s, unmarked, note difference in lid configurations, **$100-$125** each.

Two Hobnail Heart jars, in yellow and blue, early 1940s, unmarked, **$300-$350** each.

Hobnail jars, stoneware, in blue and hard-to-find coral, early 1940s, unmarked, **$100-$125** each.

Two Hobnail Heart jars in streaky blue and pink, early 1940s, unmarked, **$300-$350** each.

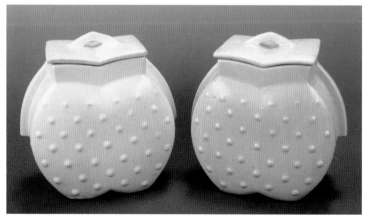

Two Hobnail Heart jars in matte white and lavender, early 1940s, unmarked, **$300-$350** each.

Hen on Nest, late 1950s, USA mark, cold-painted details, **$90-$110**.

Hocus Rabbit jar, late 1970s, also found in gray, and may be marked "McCoy USA LCC" or with Designer Accents logo, **$80-$90**.

Honey Bear jar with all decoration under glaze (some examples have cold paint), 1950s, McCoy USA mark, **$75-$90** for glazed; **$110-$125** for good cold paint.

Indian jar with cold-paint decoration, 1950s, McCoy mark, **$200-$225**. At right is a model of the Indian jar, which was used to make a block from which the mold was cast.

Two commemorative Indian jars from the 1990s (slightly smaller than the originals), made by George Williams. Rick Wisecarver of Roseville, Ohio, painted the one on the right. Left: **$150-$200**; right: **$450-$550**.

Jack-o'-Lantern jar, also comes with orange lid, late 1950s, McCoy USA mark, **$550-$650**.

Kissing Penguins or Lovebirds, in typical factory cold paint decoration, 1940s, McCoy mark, **$90-$110**. Rarely found in brown and green.

From left: Joey Kangaroo jar, late 1950s, McCoy USA mark, **$300-$350**. Blue Kangaroo, mid-1960s, USA mark, **$225-$250**.

From left: Kittens on a Basket, 1950s, McCoy USA mark, cold-painted details, seldom found without damage to ears, so beware of restorations, **$450-$550**. Kitten on Coal Bucket, 1983, McCoy USA LCC mark, also found with brown kitten on black bucket, **$200-$250**.

Kitten on Basket-weave cookie jar, 1950s, McCoy mark, 10" h, **$75-$85**.

Koala jar, 1980s, McCoy USA LCC mark, **$125-$150**.

Lamb on Basket-weave, 1950s, McCoy USA mark, cold-painted details, **$90-$110**.

Lamb on Cylinder, 1950s, McCoy USA mark, cold-painted details, **$200-$225**. Also found with cats and dogs on lid.

Lemon jar, 1970s, **$75-$85**.

Liberty Bell jar, 1960s, unmarked, more common in silver than in bronze, **$75-$90**.

Little Clown jar, mid-1940s, McCoy mark, cold-painted details, **$80-$100**.

Lollipop jar, late 1950s, McCoy USA mark, cold painted, **$70-$80**.

Lunchbox jar, late 1980s, marked Designer Accents #377 USA, **$40-$50**. Rarely found with green lid.

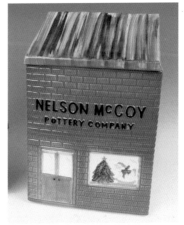

A 1999 Nelson McCoy Pottery Company jar, made in Crooksville, Ohio, as a commemorative, only 500 made, **$300-$350**.

Mammy jar in yellow, also found in white and aqua with cold-paint decoration (widely available as a slightly smaller reproduction), 1950s, McCoy mark, **$200-$225**. Rarely found with two other phrases around base: "Dem Cookies Sure Am Good" and "Dem Cookies Sure Got Dat Vitamin A."

There are many versions of the Mammy Cookie Jar, and reproductions are being made. As with many reproductions, size is the best way to distinguish the difference. The original is larger, standing 11 inches high, and noticably bigger overall. On the left is a reproduction Mammy jar; at right is the real Mammy jar with checked apron (has paint touched up), **$150-$200**.

Nabisco jar, 1974, McCoy USA mark, **$70-$100**.

Oak Leaf and Acorn corner jar (previously thought to have been produced by American Bisque), 1948, McCoy mark, **$200-$225**.

Mother Goose, late 1940s, McCoy USA mark, cold-painted details, **$90-$110**.

Nursery Rhyme canister jars, early 1970s, unmarked, including Mary Mary Quite Contrary, Little Boy Blue, Humpty Dumpty, Baa Baa Black Sheep, Little Bo Peep and Little Miss Muffet, **$75-$100** each.

Mr. and Mrs. Owl jar, 1950s, McCoy USA mark, cold-painted details, **$90-$110**.

Peanut Bird jar, late 1970s, unmarked, **$150-$175**.

Penguin jar, early 1940s, McCoy mark, typically found with worn cold paint, also found in yellow and pale green glaze, **$125-$150**, depending on paint condition.

A yellow and green Pear jar, 1950s, seen here with damage; without damage, **$125-$150**.

Two versions of the Pear jar. At left, a blushing example with strong glaze on leaf knob and minimal burgundy glaze. Right, a flat-leaf pear with strong burgundy and yellow glaze, **$125-$150**.

Lunch-hour piece, a Pear jar with a cat finial that was intended for use on a planter called "Pussy at the Well," 1950s, **$850-$1,000**.

Picnic Basket jar, early 1960s, USA mark, with cold paint on the lid, 1960s, **$90-$110**.

Big Orange jar, early 1970s, McCoy USA mark, cold-painted stem and leaves, **$90-$110**.

Two Pepper jars in yellow and green, early 1970s to about 1980, either McCoy or McCoy USA marks, lids are not interchangeable, rarely found with textured glaze, **$45-$50** each.

Rooster cookie jar with cold-painted comb and beak, 1970s, McCoy LCC mark, 13" h, **$65-$85**.

Pink Pig jar/bank, late 1970s, McCoy USA mark, **$90-$110**.

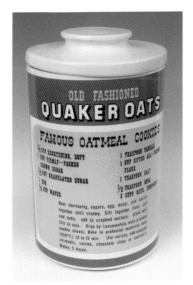

Quaker Oats jar, 1970, unmarked, not many McCoy examples, jar was later made by another company, **$500-$600**.

"Quigley" jar, also known as Lazy Pig, mid-1980s, USA mark, with original box, **$75-$100**.

Two versions of the Raggedy Ann jar, 1970s, USA mark. The one on the left is painted with typical factory colors, **$90-$110**. The jar at right was hand-painted by a McCoy employee, no established value.

Sad Clown jar, early 1970s, unmarked, cold-painted details, **$90-$110**.

Snow Bear jar, 1960s, McCoy USA mark, with cold-painted details, **$75-$85**.

Two views of a non-production Silhouette cookie jar with images of boy and girl hand-painted under the glaze (normally this form would have floral decoration), 1950s, missing lid, 6-1/2" h. No established value.

Strawberry jar, 1950s, McCoy USA mark, **$80-$100**.

Single Ear of Corn, 1958, McCoy USA mark, with good color match in the glaze, with original label, **$125-$150**.

From left: Sweet Notes jar, now acknowledged to be McCoy, though that was once in doubt, with cold-paint decoration, 1950s, **$600-$700**. Strawberries in a Basket, hard to find undamaged, late 1970s, **$150-$200**.

Two styles of the Teepee jar, late 1950s, McCoy USA mark, slant top (left) and straight top, cold-paint decoration, 11" h, **$275-$325** for slant top.

Teddy and Friend holiday variation, hand-painted at home in Christmas colors by a McCoy employee, late 1980s. Because of paint, **$175-$225**; normally **$75-$100**.

Thinking Puppy, late 1970s, USA mark, **$40-$50**. Rarely found in tan or yellow.

Touring Car in more common black and white with cold-painted details, **$100-$125**.

Touring Car jar in rare all black with gold trim, early 1960s, McCoy USA mark, **$200-$225**.

Tulip Flowerpot jar, late 1950s, McCoy USA mark, found in other color combinations, **$125-$150**.

Left: Turkey jar in white with all cold-paint decoration, 1940s, **$250-$300**, depending on paint condition. Later, in about 1960, brown with cold-painted wattle became more common. A green glaze version with no cold paint is harder to find. Right: McCoy Limited Turkey bell (part of a set of seven with varying motifs), 1990s, **$70-$80**.

Uncle Sam's Hat, mid-1970s, unmarked, hard to find, **$700-$800**.

W.C. Fields jar, 1972, USA mark, **$200-$250**.

Wedding jar, 1960s, McCoy USA mark, **$90-$110**.

Windmill jar, 1961, McCoy USA mark, note color variation between lid and jar, **$70-$110**, depending on color match.

Two versions of the Winking Pig jar, early 1970s, USA mark, typically found with cold-painted details. Yellow example is unusual, **$200-$250**.

Wishing Well jar, 1960s, McCoy USA mark, **$50-$60**.

Woodsy Owl jar and bank, 1970s, USA mark on jar, cold-painted details. Jar, **$250-$300**; bank, **$90-$110**.

Wren House jar with "V" top, in an atypical realistic glaze, early 1960s, McCoy USA mark, 9-1/2" h. As shown with V top, **$1,800-$2,000**; "V" top in normal colors, **$600-$700**.

Crocks, Churns and Jugs

Crocks, churns and jugs for use in food and beverage storage are some of the earliest examples of McCoy wares. Among the most prized pieces are those with stenciled lettering and salt-glazed surfaces; a salt glaze was applied while the ware was being fired in the kiln. A brown-colored slip glaze was used later, usually for the top half of these crocks, jugs, churns and similar items.

Nelson McCoy Sanitary Stoneware jugs, 1910-20s, shield with M mark, 2- to 6-gallon sizes, **$75-$125** depending on size.

W.F. McCoy Stoneware 2-gallon butter churn, 1850s, rare, no established value.

W.F. McCoy 1-1/2-gallon crock, salt glaze with stenciled ink lettering: "W.F. McCoy Wholesale Dealer in Stoneware– Zanesville, O.," late 1800s, 9-1/4" h, **$1,000-$1,200**.

Three brown-top miniatures: plain crock, pickling crock, and jug, range from 3" to 3-3/4" h, **$175-$225** each.

Nelson McCoy Sanitary Stoneware 6-gallon crock, 1910-1920, shield mark, came in various sizes from 2 to 50 gallons, **$100-$125**.

Nelson McCoy Sanitary Stoneware 15-gallon crock, 1910-20s, shield mark 15, **$125-$150**.

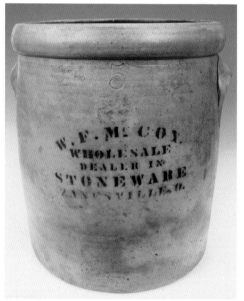

Three white crocks with stenciled shield and "M" mark, in 8-, 12-, and 20-gallon sizes, **$125-$150+**.

W.F. McCoy 5-gallon crock, salt glaze with stenciled ink lettering: "W.F. McCoy Wholesale Dealer in Stoneware–Zanesville, O.," with impressed "5," late 1800s, 13" h, **$1,200-$1,400** in mint condition.

Dinnerware

This section includes pieces used for serving, eating, and drinking. Pieces used to prepare, cook, and store food are found in Kitchenware.

McCoy manufactured a large variety of dinnerware including baking dishes, bean pots, casseroles, fondue pots, mugs, pitchers, fish-shaped serving platters, salt and pepper shakers and tea sets. As part of a Creation in Ceramics promotion, the company also created a line of Suburbia Ware that was ovenproof.

Bunnies baby set (cup not shown), late 1970s, McCoy LCC mark with serial numbers 1221 and 1222, plate 6" diameter, **$35-$40** as shown.

Bean pot, 1950s, McCoy mark, 6" h, **$65-$75**.

Two biscuit jars in glossy cobalt blue and yellow (with cold-paint stripes), 1930s, unmarked, **$75-$90** each.

Biscuit or cracker jar, glossy maroon, 1930s, **$75-$90**.

Left: biscuit or grease jar in glossy burgundy, 1950s, unmarked, **$90-$110**. Right: Suburbia creamer in glossy green, 1960s, McCoy USA mark, 5-1/2" h, **$45-$55**.

Covered casserole with Sterno burner beneath and individual French casseroles, Mt. Clemens (1967-74) mark; large casserole with cover, 8-1/2" diameter; individual casseroles, 4-1/2" diameter, **$60-$75** set.

Three different 1960s candy dishes, McCoy USA mark, **$25-$35** each.

A sampling of Canyon ware, late 1970s, included 28 pieces; for a three-piece setting, **$30-$35**.

Gorilla mug, late 1970s, McCoy LCC mark, 4-1/2" h, **$25-$35**.

J.W. McCoy mug, Carnelian glaze, gilt sponge work on handle and rim, early 1900s, unmarked, 5-3/4" h, **$150-$175**.

DINNERWARE

Cherries and Leaves serving bowl, two individual salad bowls, and two cups, all in glossy aqua, mid-1930s, unmarked, all very rare. Serving bowl, 9" diameter, **$450-$550**; salad bowls, 5" diameter, **$225-$275** each; cups, 2-7/8" h, **$90-$110** each.

Cherries and Leaves charger, 11-1/4" diameter, and individual salad bowl, 5" diameter, both in glossy yellow; bowl, **$225-$275**; charger, **$550-$650**.

Covered casserole, 1940s, McCoy USA, 6-1/2" diameter, **$55-$65**.

Covered butter dish in glossy green, 1960s, McCoy USA mark, **$30-$40**.

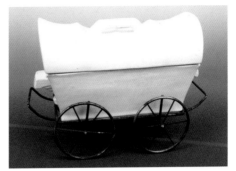

Christmas covered sugar, 1970s, **$35-$45**.

El Rancho Chuck Wagon food warmer, with wire base, 1960s, unmarked, 12" l, **$175-$200**.

Oil and vinegar cruets with original stand, mismatched stoppers, part of the "Citro-Ramics" line, early 1960s (originally sold for $1.60), McCoy USA mark, ex-Ty Kuhn collection, 9" h plus stand, **$125-$150/pair**.

Two Cloverleaf pitchers with ice lip, late 1940s, McCoy USA mark, 7" h, **$45-$55** each.

Five variations of the Smiling Face mugs, 1970s, McCoy mark, 4" h, **$15-$20** each.

Six Boy Scouts of America mugs commemorating annual events, some dated (here, 1970s), hundreds of variations with transfer decoration, **$5-$10**.

Six sports-theme mugs, late '80s, unmarked, 4" to 4-1/2" h; as a set, **$150**, but individual mugs may be valued at **$30**.

Two Bicentennial mugs, USA mark, **$15+**.

Buttermilk pitcher in glossy yellow, late 1920s, unmarked or with shield, usually found in green, sometimes in caramel-tan, 5-1/2" h, **$60-$70**.

Ball pitcher with ice lip and four goblet-style tumblers in glossy burgundy, 1940s, unmarked; pitcher, 8-1/2" h, **$50-$60**. Tumblers, 5" h, **$25-$30** each. Plus, four goblet-style tumblers in yellow, cobalt blue, aqua, and burgundy.

Ball pitcher in cobalt blue, 1940s, NM mark or unmarked, 6" h, **$50-$75**.

Elephant and Donkey pitchers (also called pitcher vases) in matte white, 1940s, NM USA mark, rare in any color, **$300-$350** each.

Two Hobnail pitchers in glossy yellow and lavender, 1940s, NM mark or unmarked, note difference in lip hole sizes, 6" h, **$50-$75** each.

Three Hobnail ice jugs, in yellow, coral, and blue, early 1940s, unmarked, **$150-$175** each.

From left: Donkey pitcher in glossy aqua, 1940s, NM USA mark, **$300-$350**. Elephant pitcher in rare burgundy, 1940s, NM USA mark, no established value.

Two Parading Ducks pitchers in glossy brown and burgundy, holds 4 pints, late 1930s, stoneware, unmarked, found in a variety of colors, **$125-$150** each.

Two Fish pitchers (also called a pitcher vase), late 1940s, McCoy mark, **$900-$1,000** each.

Miniature Pig pitchers, 1997 from the McCoy Collection, right example in non-production glaze, 6-1/2" h, **$45-$55** each.

Miniature Pig pitcher, not a production piece but marked McCoy, 5-1/2" h, **$500+**.

Three Cherries and Leaves teapots in glossy burgundy, yellow, and aqua, mid-1930s, unmarked, **$90-$110** each.

Two Parrot pitchers (also called pitcher vases), early 1950s, McCoy USA mark, **$200-$225** each.

Pitcher and two mugs in green and yellow, 1920s, stoneware, these shapes also found in barrel motif, pitcher is 9", **$100-$125**; mugs 5" h, **$30-$35** each. Also, four mugs are shown displayed in a metal rack.

Two strap-handle (also called duck's neck handle) Berry pitchers in glossy brown and green, 1930s, unmarked, **$90-$110** each.

Two Stoneware pitchers in green (common, also found in yellow) and burgundy, late 1920s, unmarked. Left: 7" h, **$65-$80**; right: 7-3/4" h, **$90-$110**.

Strap pitcher in glossy burgundy, late 1940s, McCoy mark, **$75-$85**.

Three Water Lily pitchers with Fish handles in tan and white, mid-1930s, unmarked, 7", **$85-$100**; 5-1/2", **$60-$70**; not commonly found in white.

Ring Ware pitcher and three tumblers in glossy green (note color variations), 1920s, unmarked. Pitcher, 9" h, **$80-$100**; tumblers, 4-1/4" h, **$80-$90** each.

Tall boot stein, 1970s, unmarked, 8" h, **$25-$30**.

From left: Water Lily pitcher with Fish handle in glossy green, mid-1930s, unmarked, 5-1/2" h, **$60-$70**; Bird and Cherries pitcher, mid-1930s, unmarked, 5" h, **$45-$55**.

From left: W.C. Fields pitcher (came packaged with decanter), 1970s, 7" h, **$45-$55**; non-production Grapes-motif pitcher in matte blue, marked with conjoined "TK" (Ty Kuhn), 7" h, **$50-$60**.

Soup and sandwich set, 1960s, McCoy USA on both, found in other colors, **$25-$35** set.

Soup and sandwich luncheon set in blue, 1960s, McCoy mark, plate 8-1/2" x 11", **$35-$45** set.

From left: Cabbage salt and pepper shakers with cork stoppers, 1950s, McCoy USA mark, 4-1/2" h, **$75-$85**/pair. Cabbage grease jar, 1950s, McCoy USA, 9" h, **$125-$150**.

Cucumber and "Mango" salt and pepper shakers with cork stoppers, 1950s, McCoy USA mark, 5-1/4" h, **$90-$110**/pair.

Pitcher and mugs in the Grape pattern in brown and white, late 1920s, stoneware, unmarked, commonly found in green. Pitcher, 8-1/2" h, **$80-$90**; mugs, 5" h, **$20-$25**. Produced at the same time as the Buccaneer pitcher and mugs, almost always in green with shield mark #6 on the mugs, in about the same price range.

DINNERWARE

Barrel tankard and mug in green glaze, 1920s stoneware with old circle in shield mark 4 on both pieces, 8-1/2" and 4-3/4" h; tankard, **$85-$100**; mug, **$15-$20**.

Grapes tankard and mug in green glaze, 1920s stoneware, unmarked, also found in brown and white; tankard, 8-1/2" h, **$80-$90**; mug, 5" h, **$25-$30**.

Buccaneer tankard and mugs in green and brown glaze, 1920s stoneware with old shield in circle mark; tankard, 8-1/2" h, **$75-$95**; mugs, 4-3/4" h, **$25-$30** each.

Pine Cone creamer and sugar in gold trim probably done by McCoy, 1950s, McCoy mark, **$70-$80**/pair.

Ivy teapot, creamer, and sugar in gold trim, 1950s, McCoy USA mark, rarely found in yellow and black, **$275-$325** set.

Grecian teapot, creamer and sugar, 1950s, McCoy USA mark and style number 455, teapot 8" h with lid, **$125-$150** set.

Pine Cone teapot, creamer and sugar, 1950s, McCoy mark, **$125-$150** set.

Daisy teapot with sugar and creamer, 1940s, McCoy mark, **$150-$175** set.

Experiments

Experimental pieces often served as tests for new glazes and may have inscribed number and letter codes. Though not common, they can be difficult to value since there is little basis for comparison. Still, collectors prize them as production oddities.

Tyrus Raymond Kuhn, better known as Ty Kuhn, started out painting stoneware jars and eventually became managing ceramic engineer during a 49-year career at the McCoy pottery. His collection of more than 700 pieces of pottery, including many test items and one-of-a-kind examples, was sold at auction in Roseville, Ohio, in 2002. Some of the pieces that were in his collection are featured in this section.

Left: blue and tan glaze on a baluster vase; right: part of an Apple wall pocket with burgundy glaze; ex-Ty Kuhn collection, with glaze marks, **$60-$70** each.

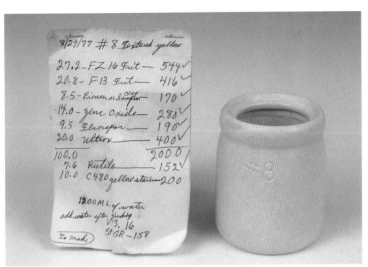

Small jar with textured yellow glaze, inscribed #8, with glaze formula written by Ty Kuhn, **$70-$90**.

Two flowerpots with speckled beige and blue glazes, inscribed on the bottom with glaze numbers, 3", ex-Ty Kuhn collection, **$50-$60** each.

Bottom of pitcher flower holder done in a test glaze with the mark, "X 79," which was a glossy coral, **$150-$200**.

Two mini jugs, the left marked "#3 bamboo," the right with eagle decal, 5-1/2" h, ex-Ty Kuhn collection, **$40-$50** each.

Left: planter in dark olive glaze, Lancaster Colony, ex-Ty Kuhn collection, **$35-$40**. Right: a pair of chafing dishes in forest green glaze, ex-Ty Kuhn collection, **$40**/pair.

Pitcher, hand-painted by Betty Ford, known for painting apples and roosters on Watt Ware pieces, 6" h, **$75**. This pitcher in factory glaze, **$45**.

Two Basket-weave pots and saucers, 3" and 4", in atypical purple and blue-green glazes, ex-Ty Kuhn collection, **$35-$40** each.

Left: pot with test glazes applied, ex-Ty Kuhn collection, 5" h, no established value. Right: money chest bank, replicating a box from the Bowery Savings Bank, late 1960s, no mark, 6" w, **$35-$40**.

Shell soap dishes in various trial glazes, with either a tripod foot or three button feet, late 1970s, **$30-$35** each.

Flowerpots

Flowerpots have a devoted following among McCoy collectors. While many pots are simple and unadorned utilitarian pieces, the challenge has become finding them in their various sizes and glazes. Many pots are unmarked, but familiarity with designs and glazes helps with attribution.

Two pots and saucers, from left: glossy turquoise, 1930s, unmarked, 6" h, **$65-$75**; Ring Ware in glossy green, 1930s, unmarked, 5-1/2" h, **$75-$85**.

Two pots in atypical glossy tan glaze, from left: 1930s, McCoy mark, 6" h, **$35-$45**; 1940s, unmarked, 4-1/2" h, **$25-$35**.

Two sizes of the "Viney" pots, one with saucer, in matte white, 1930s, unmarked, 9" h, **$125-$150**; 5" h, **$70-$80**.

McCoy flowerpot, ribbed with rose design, stoneware, 1920s, unmarked, 4" h, 5-1/2" diameter, **$30+**.

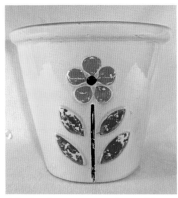

Yellow flowerpot with cold-paint decoration, 1930s, circle in shield mark 10, 6-1/2" h, **$50-$60**.

Flowerpot with attached saucer in an early Brown Onyx glaze, late 1930s, unmarked, 3-3/4" h, **$20+**.

Two Sand Dollar pots and saucers (sometimes referred to as "NECCO" style, after the round wafer cookie) in glossy green and yellow, 1930s, unmarked, 6" h, **$55-$65**; 4" h, **$45-$55**.

Lotus Leaf pot and saucer (detached) in brown and green, 1930s, unmarked, 10" h, **$350-$450**.

Three assorted pots and saucers in glossy green and yellow, and matte brown and green, 1930s, unmarked, 3" to 4" h, **$40-$60** each. The green pot is attributed to McCoy.

Four sizes of Leaf and Flowers pots and saucers in glossy burgundy, matte green and brown, and matte white, 1930s, stoneware, unmarked, 7" h, **$125-$150** (less for other matte colors); 6" h, **$65-$75**; 5" h, **$50-$60**; 4" h, **$60-$70**.

Three sizes of Ribbed pots and saucers in matte green, green and brown, and white, 1930s, unmarked, 6" h, **$90-$110**; 5" h, **$80-$90**; 4" h, **$60-$70**.

Three pots and saucers, McCoy USA marks; left and right: 3" h, **$20-$30** each; center: Icicles in blue, 6-1/2" h, **$40-$50**.

Two "Squiggle" pots and saucers in glossy yellow and matte pink, 1960s, McCoy USA mark, 5-1/2" h, **$50-$60**.

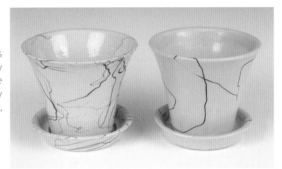

Two Green Thumb pots and saucers, 1970s, McCoy USA mark with style numbers 0375 and 0373, 6" h and 5" h, **$20-$25** each.

Matte brown pot, one with saucer, late 1970s, McCoy LCC mark, 4-1/2" and 5" h, **$40-$50**.

Four Butterfly Line pots and saucers in matte blue, aqua, coral, and yellow, 1940s, NM USA mark, 3-1/4" diameter, **$55-$65** each. Note the variation in the mold crispness; a sharp mold can add to the price.

Butterfly Line pot and saucer in matte aqua and yellow, 1940s, NM USA mark, 6-1/2" diameter, **$75-$85**. 4-1/2" h, **$45-$55**.

Two Basket-weave and Leaves pots and saucers in matte blue and yellow, 1940s, NM USA mark, 7-1/2" h, **$65-$75 each**. 5-1/2" h, **$50-$60** each.

Left: Leafy flowerpot in glossy ivory glaze, late 1940s, unmarked, 7" h, **$110-$125**. Right: Ivy pot in matte white, 1930s, unmarked, 6" h, **$50-$60**.

Two Fish-scale pots and saucers in glossy blue and yellow, 1940s, NM USA mark, 7" h, **$55-$65**; 4" h, **$40-$45**.

Three Dragonfly pots and saucers in matte blue (sometimes called "butterfly blue") and aqua, 1940s, unmarked, 3-1/2" diameter, **$60-$70**; 6" diameter, **$90-$110**; 5" diameter, **$75-$85**.

Two Dragonfly pots and saucers in matte coral and yellow, 1940s, unmarked, 3-1/2" diameter, **$60-$70** each.

Two Hobnail pots and saucers with stylized Greek key bands in glossy pink and yellow, 1940s, McCoy mark, 5" and 4" h, **$30-$40** each.

Two Hobnail and Leaves pots and saucers in matte white and blue, 1940s, NM USA mark, 4" and 3-1/2" h, **$50-$60** each.

Three sizes of Reeded pots and saucers in matte yellow, coral, and blue, 1940s, NM USA mark, 6" h, **$65-$75**; 5" h, **$55-$65**; 4" h, **$45-$55**. In semi-gloss: 6" h, **$55-$65**; 5" h, **$45-$55**; 4" h, **$35-$40**.

Three sizes of Hobnail pots and saucers in matte yellow and white, 1940s, NM USA mark, 6" h, **$90-$110**; 5" h, **$60-$70**; 3-3/4" h, **$50-$60**.

Four sizes of Flat-Leaf pots and saucers in glossy blue and burgundy, and matte green, 1940s, unmarked, 6-1/2" h, **$90-$110**; 5-1/2" h, **$80-$90**; 4" h, **$65-$75**; 3" h, **$65-$75**.

Three sizes of Lily Bud pots and saucers in matte blue, rose, and yellow, 1940s, NM USA mark, 6" h, **$65-$75**; 5" h, **$50-$60**; 3-1/2" h, **$40-$50**.

Two Leaves and Berries flowerpots in matte white, unmarked, 4-1/2" and 5" diameter, **$45-$55**.

Leaves and Berries flowerpot in matte brown and green, 5-1/2" diameter, **$60-$70**.

Two Sand Dollar pots and saucers in matte white, 1940s, unmarked, 4" and 6" h, **$40-$50** each. Note the difference in mold details: the left is crisp and the right is soft.

Two Basket-weave with Rings pots and saucers in glossy burgundy and green, 1950s, unmarked, 6" h, **$75-$85**; 4" h, **$50-$60**.

Two Brocade Line pots and saucers in pink and black and pink and green, 1950s, McCoy USA mark, 6" h, **$50-$60** each.

Garden Club pot and saucer in glossy yellow, late 1950s, McCoy USA mark, 8" h, **$80-$90**.

Left: Bulb planter (also called "the Viking helmet") in glossy white, 1950s, 5" h, **$50-$60**. Right: pot and saucer in matte white, 1930s, unmarked, 4" h, **$25-$30**.

Two Garden Club pots and saucers in matte blue, late 1950s, McCoy USA mark, 5-1/2" h, **$55-$65**; 3-1/2" h, **$45-$55**.

Two Daisy pots and saucers, 1950s, McCoy USA mark, 6-1/2" h, **$65-$75**; 4" h, **$45-$55**.

Four assorted pots in glossy cobalt blue and burgundy, matte green, and glossy yellow, 3" to 4" h, **$35-$45** each. Cobalt blue pot at left is attributed to McCoy.

Two Quilted Roses pots and saucers in glossy pink and brown, 1950s, McCoy USA mark, 5" h, **$65-$75** each.

Three Roses on a Wall pots and saucers in glossy green, 1950s, McCoy mark, also found in pink, white, and yellow, from left: 3-7/8", 5", 4-1/4" h, **$25-$45** each.

Three Quilted Rose pots and saucers in matte white, unmarked, 3", 5", and 5-1/2" h, **$40-$50** each.

Two Quilted pots and saucers in glossy blue and yellow, 1950s, McCoy USA mark, 5" h and 4" h, **$30-$35** each.

Two Icicles pots and saucers in yellow and green, 1950s, McCoy mark, unglazed border is easily soiled and tough to clean, 4-1/2" and 3-7/8" h, **$25-$30** each.

Two Swirl pots and saucers in semi-gloss green, 1950s, McCoy USA mark, 6" and 4", **$25-$35** each.

Three sizes of flowerpots in pale green, 1950s, McCoy USA mark, 7", 6-1/4", and 4-1/4", **$75-$100** each.

Two Speckled pots and saucers in glossy turquoise and pink, 1950s, McCoy USA mark, 6" and 4" h, **$25-$35** each.

Three sizes of pots and saucers in matte white and pink, early 1960s, McCoy USA mark, 6" h, **$40-$50**; 5" h, **$35-$40**; 4" h, **$30-$35**.

Pot in test glaze, ex-Ty Kuhn collection, no established value.

Pot and saucer (detached) in glossy burgundy, 1940s, unmarked, 9-1/2" h, **$125-$150**.

Large pot and saucer (detached) in glossy yellow, late 1930s, unmarked, 11" h, **$160-$175**.

Two pots and saucers (detached) in glossy cobalt blue and green, 1940s, unmarked, 6-1/2" and 5" h, **$65-$75** each.

Dragonfly flowerpots with attached saucers, 1930s-40s, NM mark; blue, 6" diameter, **$60-$70**; yellow, 5" diameter, **$40-$50**.

Two flowerpots in a skyscraper design, 1930s-40s, burgundy and yellow, also found in other colors, unmarked, 6" and 6-1/4" h, **$40+** each.

Flowerpot in a skyscraper design, with detached saucer, 1930s-40s, found in other colors, unmarked, 9" h, 10-1/2" diameter, **$75+**.

Flowerpot with attached saucer in a Blue-Brown Onyx glaze, late 1930s, impressed 5, 6" h, 5-3/4" diameter, **$30+**.

Three sizes of Hobnail and Leaves pots and saucers in glossy yellow, green, and blue, 1940s, McCoy USA mark, 6" h, **$65-$75**; 5" h, **$55-$65**; 3-1/2" h, **$45-$55**.

Three Lotus Leaf pots and saucers (sometimes saucer is detached) in glossy tan and green, matte brown and green, and glossy green, 1930s, unmarked, 6" h, **$75-$85**; 4" h, **$50-$60**.

Four textured pots and saucers in glossy pink, green, brown, and yellow, late 1950s, McCoy mark, 6" h, **$45-$55**; 5" h, **$35-$40**; 4" h, **$30-$35**; 3" h, **$20-$25**.

Three textured pots and saucers in glossy green, 1950s, McCoy mark, from left: 3", 5", and 4" h, **$25-$45** each, with the smallest being the most expensive.

Jardinières and Pedestals

From the earliest blended and matte glazes made just after the turn of the 19th century to the late incarnations of the 1970s, "jards and peds" (as collectors call them) are a challenging area for treasure hunters trying to match tops and bottoms. Many are unmarked.

Jardinière in a ring-ware design, stoneware, 1930s, unmarked, 9" h, 10" diameter opening, **$100+**.

Jardinière in a blended glaze, stoneware, early 1920s, 9" diameter, **$100+**.

Paneled jardinière in Green Onyx glaze, mid-1920s, unmarked, 8-3/4" h, **$100+**.

Miniature jardinière in Green Onyx glaze, 1930s, unmarked, 6-1/2" h, 8" diameter, **$40+**.

Jardinière in a majolica glaze, stoneware, early 1920s, 9-1/2" h, 10-3/4" diameter, **$150+**.

Butterfly jardinière, matte yellow, 7" h, NM mark, **$125-$150**.

Basket-Weave jardinière in matte aqua, 7-1/2" diameter, **$80-$100**.

Basket-Weave jardinière in matte brown and blue, 1930s, unmarked, 9" h, **$150**.

Two Butterfly jardinières in matte white, both NM mark, 3-1/2" diameter, **$30-$40**; 7-1/2" diameter, **$125-$150**.

Butterfly Line pieces in matte aqua, from left: smallest jardinière, 1940s, NM USA mark, 3-1/4" diameter, **$45-$50**. Square-top jardinière, USA mark, 3-3/4" square, **$55-$65**.

Fish in Net jardinière in rare gray-green, late 1950s, McCoy mark, also found in brown, 7-1/2" h, **$250-$300**.

Ivy jardinière in brown and green, early 1950s, unmarked, also found in a brighter glossy tan and green with matching pedestal, 8" h, **$350-$450**.

Three sizes of Hobnail jardinières in matte aqua, 1940s, NM USA mark, found in other matte colors, 3" h, **$35-$40**; 4" h, **$45-$50**; 6-1/2" h, **$75-$85**.

Three Holly jardinières in matte green: 5", **$40-$50**; 7-1/2", **$80-$90**; 4" diameter, **$30-$40**.

Leaves and Berries jardinière, Brown Onyx glaze, stoneware, 1930s, unmarked, 6-1/2" h, 7-1/2" diameter, **$50+**.

Holly jardinière in matte brown and green, 5" h, **$40-$50**. Leaves and Berries flowerpot with saucer in matte brown and green, 4-1/2" h, **$40-$50**.

Leaves and Berries jardinière in non-production pink and green glaze combination, 1930s, stoneware, unmarked, 4" h, **$75-$100** in these colors.

Leaves and Berries jardinière in matte brown and green, 1930s, unmarked, 4" diameter, **$50-$60**.

Two versions of Leaves and Berries jardinière, 1930s, stoneware, 4" diameter, unmarked, periwinkle glaze is rare, more common in brown and green and all matte green; typical colors, **$40-$50**; periwinkle, **$65-$75**.

Left and right, two 4" Leaves and Berries jardinières in matte green showing variations in color and mold crispness, 1930s, unmarked, **$35-$45**; and a 5" Holly jardinière in matte green, 1930s, unmarked, **$45-$55**.

Lily Bud jardinière, 1940s, NM USA mark, 7-1/2" diameter, **$55-$65**.

Sand Butterfly jardinière, matte yellow, 7" h, **$60-$70**.

Oak Leaves and Acorns jardinière in matte green, 5" diameter, and Holly jardinière in matte green, 4" diameter, **$40-$50** each.

Quilted jardinière in matte white, 9" diameter, **$90-$100**; Oak Leaves and Acorns jardinière in matte white, 7-1/2" diameter, **$60-$70**.

Leaves and Berries jardinière and pedestal in matte brown and green; jardinière, 7-1/2" diameter; pedestal, 6-3/4" h, **$225-$275**/ pair.

Oak Leaves and Acorns jardinière in matte green, late 1920s, unmarked, 6-3/4" h, **$70-$80**.

Sand Butterfly jardinière in matte aqua (rare color), stoneware, 1930s, unmarked, usually found white or in brown and green, 4" h, **$55-$65**.

Sand Butterfly jardinières in brown and green, 8", **$80-$90**; 5" diameter, **$40-$50**.

Leaves and Berries jardinière and pedestal in matte white, 1930s, no mark; jardinière, 7-1/2" h; pedestal, 13" h, **$350-$450**/pair. In glossy blended glazes, add **$100**.

Swallows jardinière in brown and green, stoneware, late 1930s, 7" h, 7-1/2" diameter, **$75+**.

Swallows jardinière in matte green, 1940s, unmarked, 7-1/2" diameter, **$80-$90**.

Swallows jardinières in matte white, 1940s, unmarked, 7-1/2" diameter, **$90-$110**; 4" diameter, **$50-$60**.

Sunburst jardinière in a multicolored glaze, 1930s, unmarked, 6-3/4" h, **$50-$70**.

Two hook jardinières in glossy aqua, 1940s, NM mark or unmarked, 7-1/2" diameter, **$50-$60**; 3-3/4" diameter, **$25-$30**.

Jardinière in matte aqua, stoneware, in floral pattern, 1930s, unmarked, 7-1/2" h, **$70-$80**.

Stained glass jardinière, 1950s, McCoy USA mark, 5" h, no established value.

Two hook jardinières in glossy burgundy, 1940s, NM mark or unmarked, 7-1/2", **$50-$60**; 4-1/2" diameter, **$30-$40**.

Two jardinières with applied leaves and berries, late 1940s, McCoy USA mark, 7-1/2" h, **$200-$250** each.

Basket-Weave jardinière and pedestal in matte white, jardinière 7-1/2" diameter, pedestal (NM USA mark) 13" h, **$300-$350**/pair.

Basket-Weave jardinière and pedestal, Peach glaze, late 1930s, NM USA mark, 13" and 7-1/2" h, **$250+** set.

Jardinière and pedestal in glossy turquoise and cobalt blue drip glaze, circa 1910, 41" h overall, unmarked, **$1,500-$2,000**.

Holly jardinière and pedestal in matte green, unmarked; jardinière, 7-1/2" diameter; pedestal, 13" h, **$300-$350/pair.**

Jardinière and pedestal in the Leaves and Berries pattern, Green Onyx Glaze, 1940s, 19" and 10" h, **$400-$500** set.

Quilted jardinière and pedestal in matte white, jardinière, 7-1/2" diameter, pedestal (NM USA mark), 13" h, **$200-$300**.

Leaves and Berries jardinière and pedestal in matte green; jardinière, 8-1/2" diameter; pedestal, 12-1/2" h, **$300-$400**/pair.

Leaves and Berries jardinière and pedestal in matte white; jardinière, 8-1/2" diameter; pedestal, 12-3/4" h, **$250-$300**.

Miniature jardinière and pedestal, 2000, marked, "McCoy Collection Prototype," also signed by Billie and Nelson McCoy, 4-1/2" and 9-1/2" h, **$45+** /pair.

Sand Butterfly jardinière and pedestal in matte white, 1930s, unmarked; jardinière, 9" h; pedestal, 13-1/4" h, **$300-$350**/pair.

Jardinière and pedestal in the Holly pattern, Green Onyx glaze, 1930s, unmarked, 7-1/2" and 13" h, **$225+** set.

Leaves and Berries jardinière and pedestal in matte green; jardinière, 7-1/2" diameter; pedestal, 6-1/2" h, **$225-$275**/pair.

Jars

This section includes oil jars, porch jars (basically used as big planters), and sand jars (once common in hotel lobbies as receptacles for cigars and cigarettes). Some of the larger stoneware pieces were first made in the 1920s and '30s, but these same designs can still be found on McCoy catalog pages from the 1950s.

Handled oil jar in a Green Onyx glaze, 1930s, unmarked, 19-1/2" h, **$350-$450**.

Low Sand Butterfly porch jar in matte white, 1930s, unmarked, 11" h, **$150-$200**.

Oil jar in a marbleized mauve glaze, stoneware, 1930s, unmarked, 15-1/2" h, **$250+**.

Cherries sand jar in matte white, 1930s, unmarked, 14" x 10", **$350-$450**.

Oil jar in a Blue Blended glaze, late 1930s, unmarked, 18" h, **$325-$400**.

Oil jar in glossy aqua, late 1930s, NM mark, 12" h, **$150-$200**.

Porch jar with tab handles in matte white, 1930s, unmarked, heights can vary from 17-3/8" to 18". No established value in matte white; in brown and green, **$500-$600**.

Porch jar with rings and grape motif in matte white, 1940s, NM mark, 9-1/4" h, **$175-$225**; in brown and green, **$300-$400**.

Sand Butterfly porch jar in matte white, 1930s, unmarked, heights can vary from 19-1/2" to just over 20". No established value in matte white; in brown and green, **$550-$650**.

Porch jar in matte aqua, with dense Leaves and Berries pattern and double ring handles, 1930s, unmarked, one of only three known, 11-1/2" h, **$3,500-$4,500**.

Oil jar with hand-painted floral decoration by Betty Ford, 1940s, NM mark, 12" h, with rim chip; if perfect, **$150-$200**.

Porch jar with grapes motif in matte aqua, late 1930s, stoneware, NM USA mark, 9-1/2" h, **$250-$300**.

Oil jar in a blue two-tone glaze, circa 1950s, unmarked, 18-1/2" h, **$300+**.

Kitchenware

This section includes pieces used to prepare, cook, and store food. Pieces used for serving, eating, and drinking are found in Dinnerware.

Windowpane mixing bowl in unusual periwinkle blue, 1920s stoneware, with old shield mark 7, 7" diameter, **$85-$110**.

Shoulder bowl in a windowpane pattern, 1920s, with shield mark (shown at right) and #4, 11", **$100-$125**.

Two shoulder bowls in a windowpane pattern, 1920s, with shield marks, 5", **$90-$100**, and 6", **$50-$60**.

Two shoulder bowls in a windowpane pattern, 1920s, with shield marks, 8" and 9", **$75-$85** each.

Shoulder bowl in a windowpane pattern, 1920s, with shield mark, 10", **$75-$85**.

Shoulder bowl, stoneware, 1920s, unmarked, 10-1/2" diameter, **$25-$35**.

Four mixing bowls in the Feather pattern in ivory, yellow, green, and burgundy, 1940s, McCoy mark, 6", 7", and 8" diameter, **$35-$75**.

Two square-bottom Ring ware mixing bowls in green and yellow, 1930s, shield mark with size inside (8" and 9", though they may actually be up to a half inch larger in diameter), also a pattern number (2, indicating the ring pattern), **$150-$175** each.

KITCHENWARE

Raspberries and Leaves mixing bowl in glossy white, 1930s, unmarked, 9" diameter, **$200-$225**.

Two sizes of the batter bowl with spoon rest in glossy green, late 1920s, shield mark #3, diameters without spouts and handles, 7-1/2", **$175-$225**; 9-1/2", **$275-$325**.

Mixing bowl in the Wave or Sunrise pattern, size No. 7, from a set of six ranging in size from 5" to 11" diameter, 1920s, square bottom, also found in yellow and burgundy; and three 5" mixing bowls in green, yellow, and burgundy. Complete set, about **$1,200**; individual sizes range from **$175-$250** each.

Three Raspberries and Leaves mixing bowls in teal, light burgundy, and blue, 1930s, unmarked, 9" diameter (there may be other sizes), **$200-$225** each.

Various sizes of mixing bowls with tiny berries in the outer rim and fluted bodies, 1930s, unmarked, sizes include 4", 6", 7", 8", priced in ascending sizes, **$35-$100**.

Set of four nesting ringed mixing bowls in assorted colors, 1950s-60s, McCoy Made in USA mark, 5" to 8" in diameter but came in various sizes, **$60-$80** set.

Complete set of pink and blue banded nesting mixing bowls, 1930s, old mark, 4-1/2"-11-1/2" diameter, smallest bowls are hardest to find and most expensive, **$400-$500** set.

Two mixing bowls, 1-1/2 quart and 1 pint, Lancaster Colony logo, 1970s, **$15-$25** each.

Graystone line bowl, early 1970s with Mt. Clemens mark, 8", **$15-$20**.

Five sizes of Stone Craft mixing bowls (called pink and blue) ranging in diameter from 7" to 14" (also a 5" size), mid-1970s, McCoy LCC mark. **$225-$250** for complete set.

Canister set from Fruit Festival line, 1970s McCoy mark, 12", 10", 8", 6", **$60-$75** set.

Fruit Festival line tilted cookie jar, unmarked, 9" h, **$40-$50**.

Penguin spoon rest, 1950s, 7" x 5-1/2", **$125-$175**.

Two Ring ware covered vessels (casseroles?) in glossy green, note different sized knobs, 1920s, shield mark "M"; 3-5/8" and 4" h, not including lids; **$175-$200** each.

Ring ware hanging salt box and covered jar (cheese or butter), both in glossy green, 1920s, shield mark "M." Salt box, 6" h, **$250-$300**; covered jar, 5" h, **$175-$200**.

Two Islander Line reamers in yellow and white, early 1980s, **$50-$60** each.

Lamps

Many McCoy lamp bases are unmarked, so comparing glazes can be a clue to their origin. Look for oddities, like vase forms converted to lamps, and for figural bases with atypical glazes.

Handled lamp base in Brown Onyx glaze, stoneware, late 1930s, unmarked, 9" h, **$100+**.

Lamp in Brown Onyx glaze, late 1930s, unmarked, base only 12" h, **$100+**.

"Anniversary" or Sunflower lamp base in glossy white, 1930s, unmarked, 8-1/2" h, **$50-$60**.

Arcature lamp with textured surface, 1950s, McCoy USA mark, base 9" h, **$110-$125**.

Cowboy Boots lamp, 1950s, McCoy USA mark, with replacement shade, boots only 7" h, **$75-$100**.

Two Sunflower lamps, one in blue-gray, one in burgundy, 1950s, McCoy USA mark, 9" h, **$70-$90** each. These are also found in chartreuse and yellow.

Two white Stoneware lamps, early 1940s, unmarked; left: Lily Bud pattern; right: Leaves and Berries; each 5-1/2" h, **$600-$700** each.

From left: Stoneware lamp in matte green, 1940s, 8-1/2" h, **$350-$450**. Fisherman or Whaling Man lamp base, 1950s, 16-1/4" h (reproductions are slightly smaller), **$250-$300**; more with original wiring and hardware.

Fireplace TV lamp/planter, 1950s, unmarked, also found in chartreuse and black, and with screen behind logs, 9" h, **$90-$110**.

Two Hyacinth lamps, made at the McCoy factory but not production pieces, early 1950s, McCoy mark, 8-1/2" h (pottery only), **$1,800-$2,000** each. The Hyacinth vases in these colors typically are valued at about **$150-$225**.

Mermaid TV lamp in gray and burgundy, 1950s, unmarked, also found in black and chartreuse, 9-1/2" h, **$200-$250**.

Lamp base in glossy streaked blue onyx glaze, sometimes found in matte glazes, with leafy borders and twig handles, 1940s, unmarked, 9" h, **$300-$350**.

Loy-Nel-Art

The J.W. McCoy Pottery Co. began producing Loy-Nel-Art wares in 1905. The line's distinctive title came from the names of James McCoy's three sons, Lloyd, Nelson, and Arthur. Like other "standard" glazed pieces produced at this time by several Ohio potteries, Loy-Nel-Art has a glossy finish on a dark brown-black body, but Loy-Nel-Art featured a splash of green color on the front, and a burnt-orange splash on the back.

Loy-Nel-Art low footed bowl, marked "205-8," 4" x 8-1/2", **$175-$225**.

Two Loy-Nel-Art footed jardinières, one with cherries, one with flowers, both marked Loy-Nel-Art McCoy, 5" x 5-1/2", **$200-$275** each.

Loy-Nel-Art jardinière, unmarked, 10" h, **$275-$325**.

Three Loy-Nel-Art footed jardinières with floral decoration, all marked Loy-Nel-Art McCoy, 4-1/2" h, **$175-$250** each.

Loy-Nel-Art jar with cigar decoration, unmarked, 4" x 4", **$250-$300**.

Two Loy-Nel-Art footed jardinières with flowers, marked Loy-Nel-Art McCoy, 8" and 7" h, **$325-$400** each.

Non-production Loy-Nel-Art footed jardinière, unmarked, 11" x 12", **$750-$825**.

Loy-Nel-Art pitcher, unmarked, 5-1/2" h, **$200-$250**.

Loy-Nel-Art cuspidor with pansies, marked "206," 8" h, **$200-$250**.

Loy-Nel-Art jardinière and pedestal, unmarked; jardinière, 10" h; pedestal, 18" h, **$675-$750**/pair.

Loy-Nel-Art jardinière and pedestal, unmarked; jardinière, 8" h; pedestal, 18" h, **$675-$750**/pair.

Loy-Nel-Art jardinière and pedestal; jardinière, marked Loy-Nel-Art McCoy 205, 9-1/2" h; pedestal, marked 2050, 16-1/2" h, **$1,200-$1,400**/pair.

A Loy-Nel-Art vase with tulips, left, marked "03," 10-1/2" h, **$325-$375**, is shown with the vase also at top right.

Loy-Nel-Art vase, marked Loy-Nel-Art McCoy, 10-1/2" h, **$375-$425**.

Loy-Nel-Art Greek Key vase with roses, marked Loy-Nel-Art McCoy, 10" h, **$275-$325**.

Loy-Nel-Art vase with grapes, unmarked, 12-1/2" h, **$475-$550**.

Loy-Nel-Art vase, unmarked, 7" h, **$175-$225**.

Loy-Nel-Art vase with roses, marked Loy-Nel-Art McCoy, 15" h, **$675-$750**.

Two Loy-Nel-Art vases with berries and flowers, both marked "03," 10-1/2" h, **$325-$375** each.

Two Loy-Nel-Art vases, one with pansies and one with cherries, both marked Loy-Nel-Art McCoy, 6-1/2" h, **$200-$275** each.

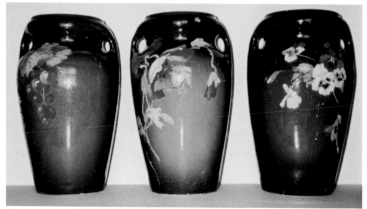

Three Loy-Nel-Art vases, with grapes, roses and pansies, all marked Loy-Nel-Art McCoy, and two also marked "02," 13" h, **$425-$500** each.

Three Loy-Nel-Art vases in different shapes, all unmarked, 8", **$175-$225**; 11-1/2" and 12" h, **$225-$275**.

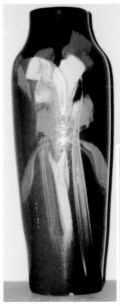

Loy-Nel-Art vase with flowers on the front and raised Indian motif on reverse, unmarked, 12" h, **$525-$575** each.

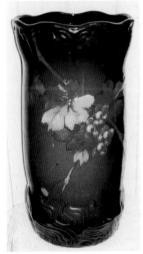

Loy-Nel-Art umbrella stand, marked Loy-Nel-Art McCoy, 21-1/2" h, **$950-$1,100**.

Pet Feeders

Some forms of McCoy pet feeders are being reproduced, and some potteries are still making dishes in vintage styles. So look for age signs like glaze crazing, discolored bases that may have an unglazed—or "dry"—foot ring, and compare weights, since old pieces are almost always heavier than later versions.

Three "Dog. (Period)" bowls, also called Spaniel feeders because the tapered design kept the dog's ears out of the bowl, 1940s, McCoy mark or unmarked, 6-1/2" diameter, **$75-$90** each.

Dog feeder, 1940s, glazed bottom, unmarked, 5" diameter, **$50-$60**.

Pet feeder, UNIPET treat bowl with bell in lid, late 1960s, UNIPET Upjohn mark, **$45-$55**.

Cat and dog feeders, 1940s, McCoy mark, 6" diameter, **$75-$90** each.

"To Man's Best Friend, His Dog" bowls showing glaze and mold variations (dry rim is earlier), 1930s and '40s, McCoy Made in USA mark, 7-1/2" diameter, **$75-$90**.

Two "To Man's Best Friend, His Dog" bowls showing bottom mark of bowls shown above. Right: reproduction bowl, 6" diameter.

Though sometimes called pet feeders, these three Stoneware dishes with Parading Elephants are also known as bulb bowls, 1920s. Green is the most common glaze (**$60-$70**; blue, **$80-$90**; yellow, **$100+**); they have an unglazed or "dry" rim, and come with two bases, low (McCoy shield mark 87) and raised with a fluted border and tripod feet (Brush McCoy, unmarked).

Two sizes of dog dishes, with decals, 1970s, McCoy Mt. Clemens mark, 7" and 6-3/4" diameter, **$90-$110** each.

Two versions of the Hunting Dog feeder with raised dog pattern, one with a dry rim and one glazed, 1930s, unmarked, 6-1/2" diameter, **$75-$90** each.

From left: new dog dish (dogs running to right, lighter weight, brighter glaze); slightly different Bird Dog dish in green glaze, 7-1/2" diameter, **$75-$90**.

Planters

Many collectors believe that planters represent the most varied and appealing area of McCoy wares. From the simple leaf forms to the elaborate figural pieces featuring birds and animals, look for examples with crisp molds and good cold-paint or gilt trim. Check closely for damage or signs of restoration, especially on planters with applied birds and flowers.

Alligator planter in gold trim, 1950s, McCoy USA, 10" l, **$125-$150**. Pedestal planter in gold trim, 1950s, McCoy mark, **$90-$110**.

Alligator planter in traditional green, 1950s, McCoy USA, 10" l, **$65+**.

Two Antelope window boxes (also called ferneries) in matte white and aqua, 1940s, NM mark (hard to find) and unmarked, come with grooved rim and without, 9-1/2" l; white, **$90-$110**; aqua, **$45-$55**.

Antelope planter, 1950s, unmarked, 12" l, **$400-$450**.

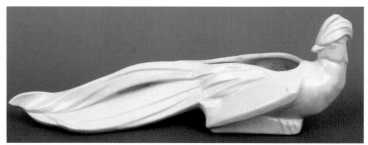

Bird of Paradise planter in glossy white (rarely found with cold-paint details), 1940s, McCoy mark, 13" l, **$55-$65**.

Bird planting dish, 1950s, McCoy mark, 10" w, **$25-$35**.

Singing Bird planter in matte white, 1940s, USA mark, found in other colors, 4-1/2" h, **$30-$40**. Also found in 6-3/4" size.

Three figural planters in glossy aqua, from left: Singing Bird, 1940s, unmarked, found in other colors, 4-1/2" h, **$30-$40**. Parrot, 1940s, NM USA mark, also found in pink and white, 7" h, **$40-$50**. Backwards Bird, 1940s, NM USA mark, also found in white and yellow, 4-1/2" h, **$60-$70**.

Caterpillar planter, 1960s, Floraline mark, 13-1/2" long, also found in brown, white, and yellow, **$40-$50**.

Two Cat with Basket planters in glossy pink and yellow, early 1940s, NM USA mark, also found in white, 6" h, **$50-$60** each.

Cat with Bow planter with cold paint decoration, 1950s, McCoy USA mark on back, 7" l, **$40-$50**.

Two Pussy at the Well planters, 1950s, McCoy USA mark, 7" h, **$125-$150**.

Three animal planters (cat with a bow, kittens with a basket, and puppy with turtle) in gold trim, 1950s, McCoy mark; kitten 7" h, **$70-$80** each.

Three animal planters—kitten, puppy, and fawn—in pearly gray and rustic brown (glazes may vary), 1970s, marks include McCoy USA LCC and USA, with serial numbers 3026, 3027, and 3028, 6-3/4" to 7-1/2" h, **$75-$90** each.

Kittens with basket planter in gold trim in another glaze combination, 1950s, McCoy mark, 7" h, **$70-$80**. Grapes planter in gold trim (rare), 1940s to '50s, McCoy USA mark, 6-1/2" l, **$275-$325**.

Bird dog planter, 1950s, McCoy USA mark, also found in chartreuse with a black or brown dog, 8-1/2" h, **$175-$225**.

Hunting dog planter in hard-to-find chartreuse glaze with black dog, 1954 McCoy mark, 12" w, 8-1/2" h, **$350-$450**.

Two Deer planters in matte aqua. Left: doe and fawn, 1940s, NM USA mark or unmarked (reissued in the 1950s in glossy yellow and green), 7" h, **$60-$70**. Right: backwards deer (one of the "ladder pieces," so named because they were pictured in an early McCoy guide on a drying rack that was tiered like the steps of a ladder), 1940s, NM mark, 4-1/2" h, **$80-$90**.

Two Dog with Blanket planters (it's actually an Airedale holding a coat in its mouth, but nobody calls it that) in aqua and blue, 1940s, NM USA mark, 5" h, **$90-$110** each.

Snooty Poodle planter (closed base, harder to find) in black with cold paint, McCoy USA mark, 7" h, **$90-$110**. Clown Riding a Pig planter with cold paint, early 1950s, McCoy USA mark, 8-1/2" l, **$110-$125**; also found with pig having raised ears, which is rare.

Flying ducks planter in natural colors, 1950s, McCoy USA mark, 10" w, **$175-$225**.

Triple Fawn planter in gold trim, 1950s, McCoy USA mark, 12" w, **$400-$450** (same price range for black and chartreuse glaze.)

Triple Fawn planter in natural colors, **$250-$275**.

Dragonfly planter with applied jewels, McCoy USA mark, 4-1/4" h, 5-3/8" w, **$80+**.

Elephant planter in matte aqua, attributed to McCoy, unmarked, 9" h, with attribution, **$100**.

Flying ducks planter in raspberry and chartreuse, 1950s, McCoy USA mark, 10" w, **$175-$225**.

From left: Swimming duck planter with cold paint, 1950s, McCoy USA mark, 7" l, **$45-$55**. Vine design planting dish with hand-painted decoration under glaze, 1950s, McCoy USA mark, 8-1/2" l, **$60-$70**.

Large Fish planter in pink, green and white, 1950s, McCoy USA mark, 12" l, **$1,200+**.

Frog with Umbrella and Duck with Umbrella planters, mid-1950s, McCoy mark, with cold-paint decoration, 7 1/2" h, **$150-$200** each.

Frog planter with worn paint, 1950, unmarked, 5" x 7-1/2", **$35-$45**.

Frog planter with worn paint, 1954, McCoy USA mark, also came in yellow, 3" x 5", **$35-$45**.

Two versions of the frog on water lily planter, 1940s, unmarked with dry bottom, 5" w, **$20-$25** each.

Frog with Umbrella planter in black (rare), mid-1950s, McCoy USA mark, with cold-paint decoration, 7-1/2" h, **$150-$200**. Carriage with Umbrella, mid-1950s, McCoy USA mark, 9" h, **$150-$200**.

Humming Bird planter in pink and green, late 1940s, McCoy USA mark, 10-1/2" w, **$125-$150**.

Cope monkey planter, cold-paint details, 1930s, 5" h, **$75+**.

Two Lamb planters in glossy black and gray, 1940s, NM USA mark, 3" h, **$55-$65** each.

Two Lion planters in matte aqua and "butterfly blue," 1940s, NM USA mark, also found in yellow and white, 8-1/4" l, **$110-$125** each.

From left: Panda and Cradle planter, 1940s, McCoy USA mark, some pandas and blankets are cold painted, 5-1/2" h, **$110-$125**. Bonnet Duck and Egg planter, 1940s, McCoy mark, cold paint, 5-3/4" h, **$175-$225**.

Panther planter in atypical glaze, usually found in green or black, unmarked, 15" l, **$65-$85** as shown; green or black, **$40-$50**.

Two Pelican and Cart planters in glossy aqua and yellow, 1940s, NM mark, 4-1/2" h, **$55-$65** each.

Pheasant planter, 1950s, McCoy USA mark, 6" h, **$70-$80**. Puppy planter, late 1950s, McCoy USA mark, 6" h, **$50-$60**.

Two Pony planters in matte aqua and yellow, 1940s, NM USA mark, 5" h, **$80-$90** each.

Quail planter in traditional colors, 1955, McCoy USA mark, 8-1/2" w, 7" h, **$80+**.

Two versions of the Rabbit planter, yellow version never had cold paint, 1950s, McCoy mark, 7-1/4" h, **$100-$150** each, depending on paint condition.

Two figural planters in matte aqua, from left: Rooster, 1940s, NM mark, 6" h, **$60-$70**. Pelican, 1940s, NM mark, 7-1/2" l, **$45-$50**.

From left: Rooster on Wheelbarrow planter in black and yellow (rare colors), mid-1950s, McCoy USA mark, 7" h, **$150-$170** in these colors. Leaf planter, 1940s, McCoy mark, 9" l, **$50-$70**.

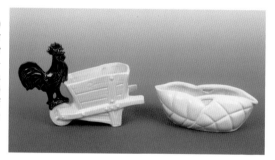

Two planters in gold trim, from left: Rooster on Wheelbarrow, mid-1950s, McCoy USA and Shafer marks, 7" h, **$200-$225**; Lamb with Bells, mid-1950s, McCoy mark, rare in gray, 7-1/2" h, **$100-$125**.

Snail planter, 1960s, Floraline mark, **$40-$50**.

Squirrel with nut planter, cold-painted details, 1950s, McCoy USA mark, 4-1/4" h, **$15+**.

Swan planter in matte aqua, 1940s, unmarked, 5" h, **$45-$55**.

Swan planting dish in chartreuse and black, 1950s, McCoy USA mark, 8-1/2" h, **$700-$800**.

Swan planting dish in rustic ivory and turquoise, 1950s, McCoy USA mark, 8-1/2" h, **$700-$800**.

From left: Swimming Swan planter with under-glaze decoration, 1950s, McCoy mark, 7" h, **$40-$50**. Harmony planting dish, 1960s, McCoy USA mark, 8-1/2" l, **$20-$25**.

Turtle planter, 1960s, Floraline mark, **$40-$50**.

Turtle planter with lily pad in atypical glaze (often found with yellow cold-paint decoration), early 1950s, McCoy mark, 8" l. Normally, **$60-$70**; as shown, **$150-$200**.

Large Turtle planter, 1950s, McCoy mark, 12-1/2" l, **$125-$150**. This is also found in other color combinations.

Large Turtle planter in dark green and pink, 1950s, McCoy USA mark, 12-1/2" l, **$175-$225**.

Stretch Dog planter (also called "angry dog"), in matte aqua, 1930s, 7-1/2" l, 5-3/4" h, **$125+**.

Stretch Cat planter, 1940s, unmarked, 4-1/2" h, **$20+**.

Small Stretch Lion in rare cobalt blue, 1940s, unmarked, 4" h, **$250-$300**.

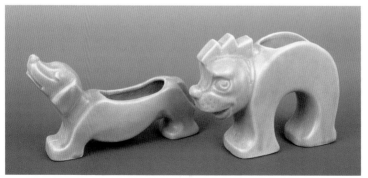

Two Stretch Animal planters, dachshund and large lion, in matte aqua, 1930s, unmarked; Dachshund, 8-1/2" long, **$150-$175**; Lion, 5-1/2" h, **$350-$400**.

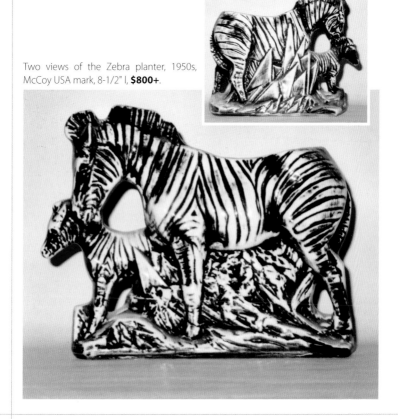

Three Stretch Animal planters (horse, butting goat, small lion), late 1930s to early '40s, unmarked, 3-1/4" to 4" h; horse, **$75-$90**; goat, **$250-$300**; lion, **$250-$300**. There are also a standing goat, a dachshund, angry dog, and larger lion in the Stretch Animals.)

Two views of the Zebra planter, 1950s, McCoy USA mark, 8-1/2" l, **$800+**.

From left: Boot and Football planter in a non-production glaze, normally found in all brown with white or yellow cold paint, 1950s, McCoy USA mark, 4-1/4" h, **$400-$450** as shown; normally **$125-$175**. Fence and Birds pot and saucer, non-production piece, 1950s, McCoy USA mark, 4-1/2" h, no established value.

Auto planter, 1950s, unmarked, 6" h, **$45-$55**.

Basket planter hand-painted by Leslie Cope, signed, 7" h, no established value.

From left: Basket planter in gold trim, 1950s, McCoy USA and Shafer mark, 9" w, **$75-$90**. Lotus form planter (also called Brown Drip centerpiece) in gold trim, 1950s, McCoy mark, 9" w, **$45-$55**.

Cowboy boots planter (this form also used for lamp base), 1960s, McCoy USA mark, 7" h, **$75-$85**.

Carriage with Umbrella planter in traditional colors, cold paint in excellent condition, mid-1950s, McCoy USA mark, 9" h, **$200+**.

Cactus flower planter, three pieces, 1950s, marked 677 USA, 7" w, **$50+**.

Left: Cornucopia planter with tassels in matte yellow, 1940s, McCoy mark, 8" h, **$55-$65**. Right: hanging basket planter, stoneware, 1930s, unmarked, 7" diameter, **$85-$95**.

Cobbler's bench planter, 1960s, McCoy USA mark, 8-1/2" l, **$45+**.

Small Cornucopia planter in gold trim, 1950s, McCoy mark, 4" h, **$40-$50**.

Two Cornucopia planters in glossy aqua and yellow, 1940s, NM USA mark, also found in white, 5" h, **$30-$35** each.

Three fruit planters—all oranges in varying glazes—1950s, McCoy USA mark, all 6-1/2" l, **$70-$90** each.

Three fruit planters—apple, pear, and grapes—1950s, McCoy USA mark, all 6-1/2" l; apple and pear, **$60-$70** each; grapes, **$150-$175**.

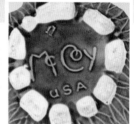

Three fruit planters—lemon, banana, and pomegranate—1950s, McCoy USA mark, all 6-1/2" l; lemon and banana, **$100-$125** each; pomegranate, **$125-$150**. The photo at right shows the McCoy USA mark and employee letter stamp, "U."

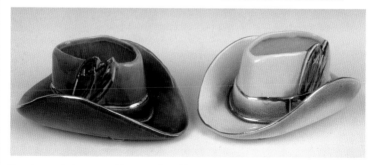

Hat planters in brown and beige with gold trim, 1950s, McCoy USA and Shafer marks, 8" l, **$60-$75** each.

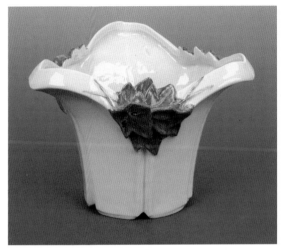

Three-sided ivy planter, 1950s, McCoy USA mark, hard to find, 6" h, **$400-$500**.

Left: Liberty Bell planter with gold trim, with 8th of July error (later corrected to 4th of July, rare), 1950s, McCoy USA mark, 8-1/4" h, **$300-$350**. Right: Quail planter in gold trim, 1950s, McCoy USA and Shafer mark, 7" h, **$125-$150**.

Liberty Bell planter with correct date and black bell in cold paint, **$350-$400**, depending on paint condition.

Two log planters, one glossy, one matte, 1970s, McCoy USA mark, each 8" l, **$25+** each.

Log planter with gold trim, 1950s, McCoy mark, also found in green, 12-1/2" l, **$110-$125** with gold trim; without, **$80-$90**.

Two small log planters in gold trim, 1950s, McCoy and McCoy USA marks, 7" and 8-3/4" l, **$35-$45** each.

From left: Mammy on Scoop planter (also found with yellow scoop), cold-paint decoration, 1950s, McCoy mark, 7-1/2" l, **$175-$200**. Boy on Rolling Pin planter (also found with yellow pin), cold-paint decoration, 1950s, McCoy mark, 7-1/2" l, **$125-$150**.

Piano planter in matte black, late 1950s, McCoy USA mark, 5" h, **$150-$175**. Tulip planter in pink and black, 1950s, McCoy USA mark, also found in green and gray, 4-1/2" h, **$60-$70**.

Two Piano planters in gold trim in white and yellow, late 1950s, McCoy USA mark, also found in matte black, 5" h, **$300-$350** each.

Old Mill planter, 1950s, McCoy USA mark, 6-1/2" h, **$90-$110**.

Rider and plow horse at trough planter, 1960s, McCoy USA mark, 8" l, 7" h, **$100+**.

Two "S" planting dishes in glossy aqua (four curving line feet) and matte white (tripod feet), 1940s, NM USA mark, note that white dish is slightly shallower, 8" l, **$25-$30** each.

From left: Rocking chair planter, with cold paint, 1950s, McCoy USA mark, 8-1/2" h, **$50-$60**. Chinaman planter, 1950s, McCoy USA mark, 5-1/2" h, **$25-$30**.

From left: Short scroll planter, 1950s, USA and Shafer marks, 4-1/2" h, **$50-$60**. Swan planter in Sunburst glaze, 1950s, "USA McCoy 192 24K Gold" mark, also with atypical pink interior, 4-1/2" h, **$100-$125**.

Sport Fishing planter with cold-paint decoration on brown bisque-style finish, from the 1956 line of sports planters, which also included a golf and bowling planter, USA mark, 6-1/4" l, **$125-$150**.

Spinning Wheel planter in traditional colors, 1950s, McCoy mark, 7-1/4" h, **$40-$45**.

Two Snowman planters with cold-painted details, late 1940s, McCoy mark, 6" h, **$70-$90**, depending on paint condition.

Trivet planter in green with mehic base, 1950s McCoy mark, 9" l, **$50-$60**.

Strawberry-form planter insert for hanging basket, McCoy 655 mark, 7" h, **$30-$40**.

Wash Tub Woman planter, not a production piece but marked NM, 6" h, ex-Cope Collection. No established value.

Two Wishing Well planters, late 1940s to early '50s, McCoy USA mark, gray and turquoise glaze is harder to find, 6" h, **$25-$35**; larger (7") size, **$55-$65**.

Two Antique Rose pieces in blue with transfer decoration: watering can and swan planter, each 7" h, 1959, McCoy USA mark, **$45-$60** each. Also found in white with red or brown rose.

Blossomtime planters in matte white, 1940s, McCoy mark, (also found in yellow), 6" and 5" h, **$50-$75** each.

Two Butterfly Line hanging basket planters in matte blue and aqua, 1940s, NM mark, found with and without holes, 6-1/2" diameter, **$200-$225** each.

Butterfly hanging basket planter in non-production dark green glaze, early 1940s, NM mark; as shown, **$500-$600;** in pastel colors, **$225-$250**.

Two Butterfly Line trough planters or window boxes in matte aqua and blue, 1940s, NM USA mark, 8-1/4" l, **$65-$75** each.

Butterfly Line window box in matte aqua, 1940s, unmarked, hard to find this size, 9-1/4" l, **$150-$175**; if marked, **$250**.

Two Butterfly Line trough planters, 1940s, NM USA mark, 5-1/2" l, **$35-$45** each.

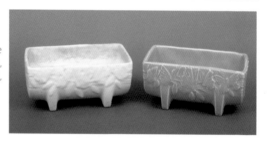

Two Butterfly Line planters in matte aqua, from left: unmarked butterfly, 1940s, 7-1/2" w, **$125-$150**. Ivy planter, 1940s, USA mark, 4" h, **$65-$75**.

Calypso Line barrel planter, late 1950s, McCoy mark, with cold-paint decoration, 5" h, **$125-$150**, depending on paint condition. Donkey with Bananas planter, 1950s, only one known to exist, 6" h, **$1,500+**.

Calypso Line Banana Boat planter, with cold-paint decoration (also found with all under-glaze color), late 1950s, McCoy mark, 11" l, **$175-$200**.

Large Centerpiece planter, 1950s, McCoy USA mark, found in other colors, 12" l, **$90-$110**.

From left: Centerpiece bowl/planter with applied bird in gold trim, 1950s, McCoy mark, 10" w, **$60-$75**. Frog and Lotus planter, late 1940s, unmarked, 4" h, **$35-$45**. Beware of reproductions.

From left: Double Cornucopia planter in gold trim, 1960s, McCoy may be visible, depending on glaze thickness, **$25-$30**. Cup planter with gold decoration, 1970s, McCoy LCC mark, **$10**.

Two Crestwood pieces, from left: Pedestal planter, 12" h; Boat planter, 13" long, mid-1960s, McCoy USA with original labels, **$60-$70** each.

Floraline rock planter, 1960s, marked "Floraline 553 Lancaster USA," 8-1/2" l, **$45-$55**.

Two Floraline planters—bear and turtle—in glossy brown glaze, 1960s, Floraline mark (may also be marked USA or McCoy), each 3-1/2" h, **$15-$20** each.

Grapes window box in matte aqua (rare), 1940s, NM USA mark, 10" l, **$110-$125**.

Grecian Line pedestal planter, 1950s, McCoy USA mark with style number 442, 8" w, **$50-$60**.

Grecian Line window box, 1950s, McCoy USA mark with style number 435, 12" l, **$85-$95**.

Two Harmony boat planters, early 1960s, McCoy mark, also found in orange and a brighter yellow, 8-1/2" and 9 1/2" l, **$25-$30** each.

From left: Harmony boat planter in gold trim, 1960s, McCoy USA mark, 12" l, **$40-$50**. Crestwood footed planter, 1960s, McCoy USA mark, 4-1/2" h, **$40-$50**.

From left: square-top Hobnail planter in matte aqua, 1940s, NM USA mark, 4" h, **$55-$65**. Ball planter in glossy aqua (also called rose bowl), 1940s, NM USA mark, 3-1/2" h, **$45-$55**.

Small Hobnail planter in matte aqua, early 1940s, unmarked, probably a cut-down vase, 3-1/4" h, no established value.

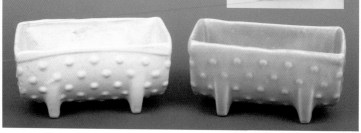

Two Hobnail trough planters in matte white and aqua, 1940s, NM USA mark, 5-1/2" l, **$30-$40** each.

Two Hobnail trough planters in matte blue and aqua, 1940s, NM USA mark, 8-1/2" l, **$50-$60** each.

Icicles window box, 1950s, McCoy USA mark, 8-1/2" l, **$70-$80**. Garden Club pedestal planter, late 1950s, McCoy USA mark, 7" h, **$40-$50**.

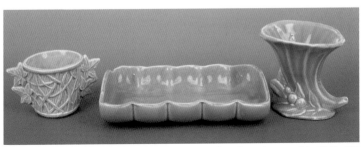

From left: Ivy planter, 1950s, McCoy USA mark, 3" h, **$30-$40**; planting dish, 1940s, NM USA mark, 9" l, **$35-$45**; small Cornucopia planter, 1950s, unmarked, 4-1/2" h, **$35-$45**.

Jewel Line planter with applied butterflies, 1950s, 4-1/4" h, McCoy USA mark, **$100+**.

Three Jeweled Line planters in gold trim, 1950s, McCoy USA and Shafer marks, one with dragonfly, decorated with rhinestones (often missing), 7-1/2" and 8-1/2" w; dragonfly, **$150-$200;** others, **$90-$110** each.

Large Leaf planter in matte green, 1930s, stoneware, unmarked, 6-1/2" h, **$80-$90**. This form was reissued in the 1950s as part of the Garden Club Line.

Large Leaf planter in brown and green, 1930s stoneware, unmarked, 10-1/2" l, **$65-$75**.

Leaves and Berries hanging basket planter in matte aqua, 1930s, unmarked, 6" h, **$50-$60**.

Leaves and Berries hanging basket planter in matte green, 1930s, unmarked, 5-1/4" diameter, **$60-$70**.

From left: Leaves and Berries planter with hand-painted decoration under glaze, 1950s, McCoy USA mark, 5" h, **$45-$55**. Wheat vase, 1950s, McCoy mark, 8" h, **$55-$65**.

Lily Bud divided planting dish in matte aqua, 1940s, NM USA mark, 11-1/2" l, **$85-$95**.

Two Lily Bud planting dishes in matte aqua, 1940s, NM USA mark, from left: 9" l, **$65-$75**; 8" l (called the cross), **$65-$75**.

From left: Lily Bud "twig" planter in matte aqua, 1940s, NM USA mark, 5" h, **$90-$110**. Lily Bud "banana boat" planter in matte aqua, NM USA mark, 8-1/2" l, **$55-$65**.

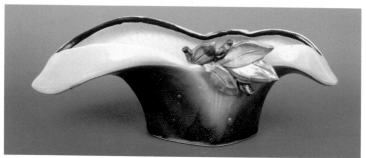

Fancy Lily Bud planting dish, late 1940s or early 50s, hand-painted under glaze, 11" l, **$85-$95**.

Lily Bud divided planting dish in matte blue, 1940s, NM USA mark, 6-1/2" w, **$65-$75**.

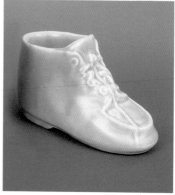

Mary Jane shoe planter in matte aqua, 1940s, NM USA mark, **$35-$45**.

Lotus leaf planter in gold trim, 1950s, McCoy USA mark, 4-1/2" h, **$50-$60**. Water Lily planter, 1950s, McCoy USA mark, also found in green and rarely in orange, 3-1/2" h, **$100-$125**.

Two Bear and Ball planters, part of the Nursery line, late 1940 or early 50s, with cold paint, McCoy USA mark, 5-1/2" h, **$125-$150** each.

Two Baby Buggy planters (called "What About Me?") in gold trim, part of the Nursery Line, 1950s, McCoy USA mark, 6" h, **$125-$150** each; without gold trim, **$70-$80**.

Two Nursery Line planters, from left: Dog with Cart, 1950s, McCoy USA mark, 8-1/2" l, **$45-$55**. Lamb with Bow, 1950s, McCoy USA mark, with cold paint, 8-1/2" l, **$45-$55,** depending on paint condition.

Baby Crib planter, part of the Nursery Line, 1950s, unmarked, 6-1/2" l, **$30-$40**.

Four Nursery Line planters, all came with cold-paint decoration,1950s,unmarked: Lamb with block, 4-1/2" h, **$55-$65**; Baby scale, 5-1/2" h, **$35-$45**; Rattle, 5-1/2" l, **$70-$80**; Raggedy Ann and blocks, 5-1/2" h, **$75-$85** (prices vary depending on paint condition).

Two Nursery Line planters, from left: Rabbits and Stump in yellow and blue (rare), also found in brown and yellow, and rustic ivory and brown, 1950s, McCoy USA mark, as shown, **$150-$175**. Lamb with Two Bells planter in rare gray, 1950s, McCoy mark, 7-1/2" h, **$125-$150**.

Ba Ba Black Sheep planter, part of the Nursery Line, 1930s, NM USA mark, also found in yellow, blue, and white, **$50-$60**.

Two Rocking Horse planters, one in gold trim, one plain yellow (rare), part of the Nursery Line, 1950s, McCoy USA and Shafer mark. Gold trim, **$200-$225**; yellow, **$225-$250**; in pink or green, **$125-$150**.

Two Stork planters in gold trim, part of the Nursery Line, 1950s, McCoy USA and Shafer marks, rare in yellow, 7" h, **$110-$125** each.

Stork planter in green, part of the Nursery Line, 1950s, McCoy USA mark, 7" h, **$110-$125**. Snooty Poodle planter (pierced base), 1950s, McCoy USA mark, also found in green and commonly in black, 7" h, **$75-$90**.

Oak Leaf and Acorn basket in matte white, early 1950s, McCoy USA mark, **$60-$70**.

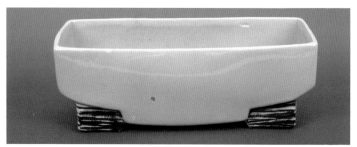

Pedestal Line window box or planting dish, 1959, McCoy USA mark, 11" w, **$35-$40**.

Petal basket planter, 1950s, McCoy USA mark, 8-3/4" h, **$150-$175**.

Two Petal basket planters (uncommon in darker glazes at left), 1950s, McCoy USA mark, 8-3/4" h; darker, **$110-$125**; lighter, **$75-$90**.

Pine Cone planter, mid-1940s, McCoy USA mark, 8" wide, rare, **$500-$600**. (A slightly larger planter in rust glaze, **$1,800-$2,000**)

Rustic Line planter with seven wide-eyed animal faces (probably intended to be fawns) peering out of the foliage, called by some collectors "the devil dog planter" or "gremlins planter," 1940s, McCoy mark, 6" h, **$60-$70**.

Two Sand Butterfly trough planters in matte aqua and glossy coral, 1930s, USA mark, 8-3/4" l, matte colors, **$50-$65**; coral, **$65+**.

From left: Sand Butterfly planter (also called a fern box) in gold trim, 1940s, McCoy USA mark, found in other pearly colors, 8-1/2" l, **$45-$55**. Scallop-edge planter in gold trim, early 1960s, McCoy USA mark, 9" l, **$35-$45**.

From left: Scoop planter in forest green, late 1950s, McCoy mark, 6" w, **$25-$35;** low Vine planter with under-glaze decoration, mid-1950s, McCoy mark, 8 1/2" w, **$35-$45**.

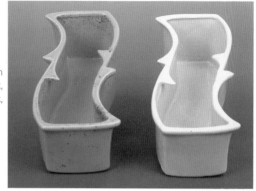

Two Spiked planters in matte aqua and pink, 1950s, McCoy USA mark, 9" l, **$50-$60** each.

From left: Strawberry planter in matte blue, stoneware, 1930s, unmarked, 6-1/2" h, **$85-$95**. Shell planter in matte aqua, also found in glossy colors, 1940s, NM USA mark, 7-1/2" l, **$55-$65**.

Two forms of Strawberry planters, one in atypical dusty burgundy, one in glossy green, stoneware, 1930s, unmarked, 7" h, **$60-$70** each. This form is also found with a raised leaf motif on the body, called style #2.

Village Smithy planter in gold trim, 1950s, McCoy USA mark, 6-1/2" h; spinning wheel planter with cat and dog, 1950s, McCoy mark, 7-1/4" h, **$90-$110** each.

Village Smithy planter in atypical burgundy and gray (usually in brown and green), 1950s, McCoy USA mark. As shown, **$300-$350**; in common glaze, **$70-$80**.

Water Lily planter with tan details, normally found in all green and yellow, 1950s, unmarked, 7-1/4" l, **$50-$60**.

Two Wild Rose planters in matte yellow, 1950s, McCoy mark, 8-1/4" w, **$60-$75**; 6" h, **$45-$55**.

Zigzag planting dish in matte aqua, 1940s, NM USA mark, 9-1/2" l, **$110-$125**.

Ball planter in gold trim (also called rose bowl), 1940s, NM USA mark, 3-1/2" h, **$45-$55**. This form also comes in a 7" h size with a McCoy mark, **$70-$80** in gold trim.

Ball planter (also called rose bowl), 1940s, NM mark, 3-1/2" h, **$35-$45**. This form also comes in a 7" h size with a McCoy mark, **$60-$70**. The shorter size was a popular choice for glaze tests and may be found with inscribed glaze numbers.

Two hanging basket planters, in brown and green and matte white, 1930s, unmarked, 6" diameter. **$70-$90** each.

Two garden dishes or window boxes in matte blue and aqua, early 1940s, NM USA mark, rare, 9-1/4" l, **$110-$125**.

Low planting dish with drape design in matte aqua, 1940s, NM USA mark, 8-1/2" diameter, **$65-$75**. This is rarely found without an inverted lip.

From left: round planting dish, McCoy mark, 7" diameter, **$25-$35**. Window box, McCoy USA mark, 8-1/2" l, **$35-$45**.

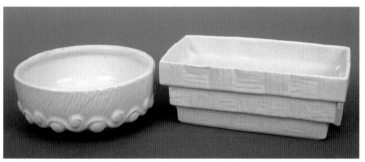

Round planting dish in matte aqua, late 1940s, McCoy mark, 8-1/4" diameter, **$35-$45**.

Single cache planter in black and pink, 1950s, McCoy USA mark, 9" w, **$70-$80**.

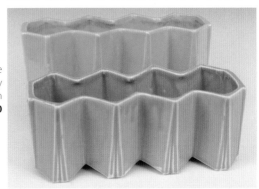

Two jagged edge planters, 1950s, McCoy USA mark, also found in yellow, 10" l, **$150-$200** each.

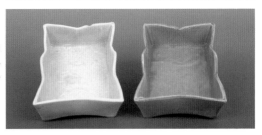

Two planting dishes in matte pink and aqua, 1940s, NM USA mark, 9" l, **$35-$40** each.

Left: small fin planter, early 1950s, USA McCoy mark, 3-1/2" h, **$50-$60**. Right: Trinket box in unusual brocade glaze, 1960s, McCoy USA 464 mark, 3-1/2" h, **$70-$80**.

Small planter usually found in pink or blue, with under-glaze decoration, 1940s, 5" h, **$45-$55**.

Planter with stand, 1950s, McCoy USA mark, 7" l, **$35-$45** with stand, which is often missing.

Left: planter, came with metal stand, 1950s, McCoy USA mark, **$25-$35** with stand. Right: planting dish, 1940s, McCoy mark, **$35-$45**.

Two planters, from left: 1950s, McCoy USA mark, 9" l, **$25-$35**; 1940s, McCoy USA mark, 8-1/4" l, **$55-$65**.

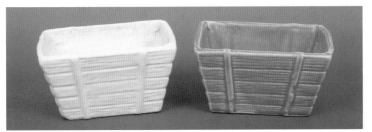

Two small trough planters in glossy white and aqua, late 1950s, USA mark, 6" w, **$20-$25** each.

Pair of ribbed and footed planters in matte white, late 1940s, unmarked, 6" h (also come in 8" size), **$70-$80**/pair.

Stump planter with more common "ST-VH" initials in glossy brown, 1950s, McCoy mark, also found in yellow and green, 4" h, **$25-$35**. Ducks and eggs planter in purple glaze (rare color), 1950s, McCoy USA mark, 5" h, **$55-$65** in this color; otherwise, **$30-$40**.

Square textured planters in glossy green, interlocking, 1950s, unmarked, 3-1/2" and 5" h, **$25-$30** each.

Triple Pot planter in gold trim, 1950s, McCoy USA mark, 12-1/2" l, **$200-$225**.

Stump planter with rare "Ted & Anne" theme, 1950s, McCoy mark, also found in yellow and green, 4" h, **$60-$70**. Swans planter in green, 1950s, McCoy mark, common in white and yellow, 8-1/2" l, in green, **$30-$40**.

Triple bulb bowl in pink and black, 1950s, McCoy mark, 8" w, **$165-$185**.

Signs

Block used to make the mold for "The Pottery Shop by McCoy" signs. No established value.

Two McCoy Pottery signs, from left: sign intended for use at JC Penney stores, 4" x 5-1/4", **$400-$450**. Contemporary sign by Billie and Nelson McCoy, 4" x 5-1/4", **$250-$300**.

McCoy Pottery sign, contemporary, by Billie and Nelson McCoy, signed and dated 2001, 4-1/2" x 8-1/2", **$40-$50**.

Vases and Flower Holders

Second only to planters in their variety, McCoy vases also present special challenges because many of them lack formal names. Collectors use descriptions like "the vase with the low drape handles" or "the one that looks like a chevron." Others define collecting areas based on glazes (matte aqua or the glossy palette) and seek examples in the smaller sizes.

Patterned flower bowl in a swirl glaze, stoneware, mid-1930s, unmarked, 8" diameter, **$50+**.

Two flower frogs, stoneware, 1920s, duck in a blended glaze, fish marked 063, each 4-1/4" l, **$35+** each.

Three small flower holders in glossy white, pink, and yellow, 1930s, NM mark or unmarked, 3-1/4" h, **$60-$70** each. McCoy matte colors include aqua, blue, lavender, white, yellow, and brown and green.

Three miniature flower holders in Sunburst gold (the Cornucopia and Swan are "ladder pieces," so named because they were pictured in a early McCoy guide on a drying rack that was tiered like the steps of a ladder), 1940s to 1950s, unmarked, 3-1/4" h, **$60-$70**, depending on color.

Six miniature Cornucopia flower holders in matte colors, 1940s, NM USA mark, 3-1/4" h; blue, white, aqua, **$50-$60**; pink and yellow, **$125-$150**; coral, **$175-$225**.

Three Pigeon or Dove flower holders (called "ladder pieces," so named because they were pictured in a early McCoy guide on a drying rack that was tiered like the steps of a ladder), 1940s, USA mark, 3-1/2" h, 1940s. **$100-$125** each.

Three Pitcher flower holders, 1940s, NM USA mark, 3-1/4" h; in pink, blue and yellow, **$80-$90** each.

Three Fish flower holders (one of the "ladder pieces," so named because they were pictured in an early McCoy guide on a drying rack that was tiered like the steps of a ladder), 1940s, NM USA mark, 3-1/4" h, **$90-$125**, depending on color.

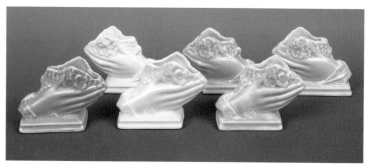

Six Praying Hands flower holders, 1940s, NM USA mark, 3" h, **$100-$125** each except for white and aqua, **$50-$60**.

Five Turtle flower holders (also called miniature planters), 1940s, NM USA mark, 4-1/4" l; aqua and white, **$40-$50**; blue, **$70-$80**; pink and yellow, **$125-$150** each.

Five Swan flower holders in matte colors (called "ladder pieces," so named because they were pictured in a early McCoy guide on a drying rack that was tiered like the steps of a ladder), 1940s, NM USA mark, 3-1/4" h, usually **$60-$70**, but yellow and pink (the only one found in glossy finish) may bring **$100-$125**.

Miniature Vase flower holder, at top, NM mark, 3" h, **$55-$65**. Miniature Turtle flower holder (one of the "ladder pieces," so named because they were pictured in a early McCoy guide on a drying rack that was tiered like the steps of a ladder), 1940s to 1950s, NM mark, 4" l, **$80-$100**.

Cat vase in matte black (also found in white and gray), 1960s, McCoy USA, 14" h, **$225-$250**. Antique Curio Line vase in glossy brown (also found in green and white), 1960s, McCoy USA mark, 14-1/2" h, **$110-$125**.

Antique Curio Line gladiolus vase in traditional colors, style #1607, late 1950s, McCoy USA mark, 14-1/4" h, **$85+**.

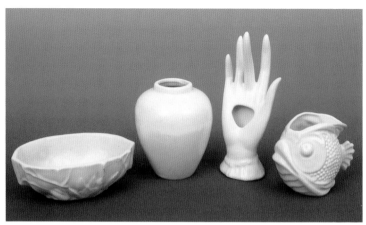

From left: Lily Bud pin dish, NM mark, 5-1/2" w, **$40-$50**; miniature oil jar, 4-1/4" h, **$40-$50**; small hand vase (fingers separated), 6-1/2" h, **$100-$125**; fish flower holder (one of the "ladder pieces," so named because they were pictured in an early McCoy guide on a drying rack that was tiered like the steps of a ladder), 1940s to 1950s, 3-1/4" h, **$90-$125**, depending on color.

Arrow leaf vase in Rustic glaze, McCoy mark, 10" h, **$125-$150**.

Arcature vase in atypical dark lavender glaze (usually green and yellow), early 1950s, McCoy USA mark, 6-3/4" h; in normal colors, **$50-$60**; as shown, **$150-$200**.

Antique Rose low flower bowl in blue with transfer decoration, 1959, McCoy USA mark, 12" w, **$55-$65**. Also found in white with red or brown rose.

Two Antique Rose pieces in blue with transfer decoration. Flower bowl, 9-1/2" w, and pitcher vase, 9" h, 1959, McCoy USA mark, **$45-$55** each. Also found in white with red or brown rose.

Two Arrow Leaf vases in matte aqua and coral, 1940s, McCoy mark or unmarked, 7-1/2" h, **$85-$95** each.

Bird of Paradise vase with cold paint decoration (not factory), found in glossy colors, late 1940s, unmarked, 8-1/4" h, **$40-$50**.

Two Baluster vases in matte white, 1940s, unmarked, heights vary from 12" to almost 13"; with handles, **$150-$175**; without handles, **$200-$250**.

Two gold trim vases, from left: Bird and Berries, 1950s, McCoy USA mark, 8" h, **$125-$150**. Petal vase (also called Celery vase), 1950s, McCoy USA mark, 9" h, **$250-$300**.

Blossomtime handled vase, 1940s, raised McCoy mark, 6-1/4" h, **$100+**.

Blossomtime rectangular vase, 1940s, raised McCoy mark, 8" h, **$100+**.

Blossomtime vases in yellow, 1940s, McCoy mark, one matte, one glossy, 6-3/4" h, **$70-$80; 8" h, $60-$70.**

Two Blossomtime vases, 1940s, McCoy mark, 6-1/2" h, **$50-$60** each.

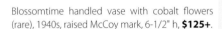

Blossomtime handled vase with cobalt flowers (rare), 1940s, raised McCoy mark, 6-1/2" h, **$125+.**

From left: Blossomtime vase in atypical glaze (white flower), mid-1940s, McCoy mark, 8" h, **$100-$150**; non-production vase with applied berries and leaves, hand cut from a taller vase, ex-Cope Collection, 5" h, no established value.

Three Butterfly Line vases in matte blue, yellow, and white, from left: cylinder vase, 1940s, NM USA or NM mark, 8" h, **$75-$85**; two-handled vase, 1940s, USA mark, 10" h, **$200-$225**; cylinder vase, NM mark, 6" h, **$55-$65**.

Two Butterfly Line "V" vases in matte blue and yellow, 1940s, NM USA mark, 9" h, **$90-$110**.

Butterfly cylinder vase with under-glaze decoration, 1940s, NM mark, 8" h, **$350-$450**; in typical colors of coral, yellow, blue, or green, **$60-$90**.

Large Fan vase, also called "Blades of Grass," glossy black, late 1950s, McCoy USA mark, 10" h, **$175-$225**.

Two Butterfly Line, Castle Gate or "Binoculars" vases, 1940s, USA mark or unmarked, found in other matte colors, 6" h, **$185-$215** each.

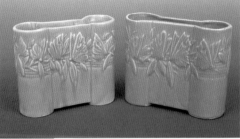

Two Butterfly Line vases, from left, matte blue pitcher, 1940s, NM USA mark, 10" h, **$175-$200**; cylinder vase in matte aqua, 1940s, NM USA mark, 6" h, **$55-$65**.

Classic Line bud vases, early 1960s, McCoy USA mark, 8" h, **$35-$45** each.

Square Cherry vase, stoneware, 1930s, unmarked, **$100-$125**.

Garden Club vase in matte yellow, late 1950s, McCoy USA mark, 9-1/2" h, **$150-$175**.

Two Floraline vases in matte white, 1960s, both marked Floraline USA, 10" rectangular vase, **$45-$55**; 3-1/2" chalice, **$15-$20**.

Two Drape-handle vases in matte white, 1940s, unmarked, also found in 6", 8", and 10" sizes, and glossy green, blue, and yellow, 12" h, **$90-$110**; 9" h, **$60-$75**.

Grecian urn vase, 9-1/2" h, 1950s, **$110-$125**.

Left: Hobnail "V" vase in matte blue, 1940s, NM USA mark, 9" h, **$110-$125**. Center and right: two Hobnail vases in matte aqua, 6" and 8", 1940s, NM USA mark; 6", **$55-$65**; 8", **$90-$110**.

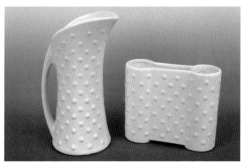

From left: Hobnail pitcher vase in white, 1940s, NM USA Mark, 10" h, **$125-$150**. Hobnail castle gate or "binoculars" vase in white, 1940s, unmarked, 6" h, **$175-$200**.

From left: Hobnail and Leaves vase in glossy aqua, 1940s, NM USA mark, 7" h, **$75-$85**. Ring ware vase with handles in glossy green, 1940s, McCoy USA mark, 5-1/2" h, **$50-$60**.

From left: Leafy vase in matte white, 1940s, unmarked, 7-1/2" h, **$100-$125**; two Arrow Leaf vases in matte white, 1940s, unmarked, 10" h, **$125-$150**; 8" h, **$90-$110**.

Ivy vase (also called English Ivy) in an atypical maroon and yellow, hand-painted, (normally white or yellow), 1950s, McCoy mark, 9" h; as shown, **$800+**; white or yellow, **$125-$150**.

From left: Leaves and Berries Hourglass vase in matte green glaze, 1930s, stoneware, unmarked, 14" h, **$400-$450**. Stoneware Urn vase in glossy green glaze, hard-to-find form, 1930s, unmarked, 8" h, **$250-$275**.

Two Leaves and Berries fan vases in white and burgundy, 1940s, burgundy with round McCoy USA mark, white with McCoy USA mark, 6" h, **$70-$90** each.

Three vases in blue, from left: Double Bud vase in glossy cobalt, 1940s, NM mark, also found in aqua, dark green, turquoise, and yellow, **$75-$90**; Stoneware vase in blue with "flat flower," 1930s, unmarked, 7" h, **$175-$200**; two-handled vase in cobalt, 1950s, unmarked, 7" h, **$40-$50**.

Three Leaves and Berries fan vases, commonly found in aqua, pink, white and yellow; cobalt blue is hard to find, and the under-glaze decorated example at left is very rare; late 1930s or early '40s, McCoy USA or unmarked, 6" h, from left: **$175-$200**; **$110-$125**; **$75-$90**. Beware of reproductions, which are lighter, have soft mold details, and thinner glazes.

Three Leaves and Berries footed vases in different glaze combinations, rare in blue and all white, 1930s, stoneware, unmarked, 7" h; typical colors, **$50-$75**; blue/white, **$75-$125**.

Leaves and Berries urn-form vase in matte white with small handles and unusual interior ring pattern, hard to find form, stoneware, 1930s, 8" h, **$300-$350**.

Leaves and Berries vase in matte brown and green, and Cornucopia vase in semi-gloss brown and green, stoneware, 1930s, unmarked, each 8" h, **$70+** each.

Leaves and Berries vase in matte brown and green, unmarked, 7" h, **$80-$90**.

Two Leaves and Berries vases (sometimes called the stovepipe), 1930s, unmarked, in what McCoy called "onyx" glazes, 8" h, **$80-$90** each.

Three Leaves and Berries vases with tab or ear handles in matte white, 1930s, unmarked, 5" h, **$80-$90**; 8" h, **$90-$110**.

Left: Lily Bud pillow vase in matte white, 1940s, NM mark; right: Heart vase in matte white, 1940s, unmarked, each 6" h, **$60-$70** each.

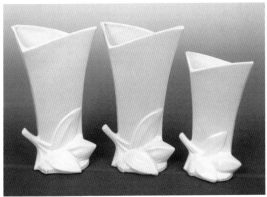

Three Lily Bud vases in matte white and yellow, 1940s, NM USA mark (also found unmarked), 8" h, **$80-$90** each; 10" h, **$125-$150** each.

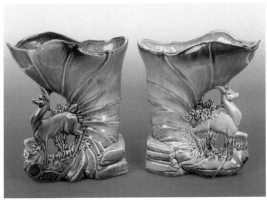

Two Deer and Cornucopia vases, 1950s, McCoy USA mark, 9" h, example at right is in rare brown and green. Left: **$70-$80**; right: **$125-$150**.

Phial vase in dusty pink, mid-1980s, Designer Accents with USA and 44 mark, 12" w, **$25-$30**.

J.W. McCoy Olympia vase, with rare cream-drip glaze overflow, early 1900s, marked 28, 5-1/4" h, **$195-$225**.

Pine Cone vase, not a production piece, mid-1940s, McCoy USA mark, 9-1/2" h, **$800-$1,000**.

Three Stoneware Hourglass vases in matte white, 1930s, unmarked, also found in yellow, pink, varying shades of green, and brown and green, 12" h, **$200-$225**; 8" h, **$90-$110**; 6" h, **$75-$90**.

Ribbed vase in atypical brown glaze, 1940s, unmarked, 6-1/2" h, **$55-$65**.

Ring ware vase, 1920s, unmarked, 9-1/4" h, **$100-$125**.

Two Ripple Ware vases in gold trim, glossy yellow and turquoise, early 1950s, McCoy mark, also found in other colors with dripping glazed rims, 7" h, **$90-$110** each.

From left: Grape vase in gold trim, 1950s, McCoy USA mark, also found with brown and green glazes, 9" h, **$90-$110**. Sunburst gold vase, 1950s, faint McCoy USA mark, 6" h, **$60-$75**.

Sand Dollar vase in matte white, stoneware, 1940s, unmarked, also found in pastel colors, and brown and green, **$250-$300**, depending on color.

Scandia Line floor vase, 1970s, McCoy LCC mark, 14-1/2" h, **$45-$55**.

From left: Tassel vase in glossy raspberry, 1930s, stoneware, unmarked, 8" h, **$75-$85**. Flower pot with cold-paint decoration, 1940s, shield mark 10, 6" h, **$85-$95**.

Vesta line vase, 1962, McCoy mark, 8-1/2" h, **$25-$35**.

Two Wild Rose vases with atypical glaze combinations, usually blue, lavender, pink, and yellow (with pink flowers), early 1950s, McCoy mark; in these colors, **$175-$200** each; in common colors, **$80-$100** each.

Two Chrysanthemum vases in atypical glazes, early 1950s, McCoy mark, 8-1/4" h; left: **$150-$200**; right: **$275-$300**.

Single Lily bud vases, usually white or yellow with decoration under glaze, late 1940s, McCoy mark, 8" h, **$90-$110** each.

From left: large Lily vase in gold trim, mid-1950s, McCoy mark, 8-1/2" h, **$700-$800**; rare Tulip vase in air-brush decoration, 1950s, McCoy mark, 8-1/4" h, **$800-$1,000**.

Hyacinth vases in a range of glazes, early 1950s, McCoy mark, 8" h, **$150-$225** each, depending on glaze intensity and mold crispness.

Two Large Lily vases in typical glazes (blue leaves are matte, green are glossy), mid-1950s, McCoy mark, 8-1/2" h, **$500-$600** each.

Triple Lily vases, one with original paper label, seen in matte white and glossy yellow, also comes in glossy white, early 1950s, McCoy mark, 8-1/2" h, **$100-$125** each.

Two Magnolia vases, with the example on the left having the more typical glaze combination, early 1950s, McCoy mark, 8-1/2" h, **$250-$300** each.

Two gold trim vases, from left: Magnolia, 1950s, McCoy USA mark, 7-1/2" h, **$250-$300**. Hyacinth, 1950s, McCoy USA mark, slightly duller gold finish, 8" h, **$400-$425**.

Poppy vase in gold trim, 1950s, McCoy mark, reverse not gold trimmed, 8-1/2" w, **$1,000-$1,200**.

Pink Poppy vases show a variation in glaze intensity, Mc-Coy mark, 8-1/2" w, **$350-$450** each.

Two Poppy vases in pink and yellow (harder to find), mid-1950s, McCoy mark, **$800-$1,000** each, depending on glaze intensity and mold crispness.

Two gold trim vases, from left: Sunflower, 1950s, unmarked, 9" h; ewer with hand-painted grapes under glaze, late 1940s, initialed W, 9" h, **$150-$175** each.

Sunflower vase using same mold as lamp, 1950s, with unusual airbrush decoration, unmarked, **$450-$550**.

Fawn vase and Chicken pitcher vase (also with floral decal) in gold trim, 1950s, McCoy and McCoy USA mark; fawn vase, 9" h, **$125-$150**; chicken, **$90-$110**.

Tall Double Tulip vases in a range of glazes, late 1940s, McCoy mark, 8" h, **$100-$125** each.

From left: Low Double Tulip vase in gold trim, early 1950s, McCoy USA mark, 6-1/2" h, **$325-$375**. Magnolia vase in gold trim, early 1950s, McCoy mark, 8-1/2" h, **$350-$400**.

From left: Low Double Tulip vase in gold trim, early 1950s, McCoy USA mark, 6-1/2" h; Triple Lily vase with gold trim, early 1950s, McCoy mark, 8-1/2" h, **$175-$225**.

Heart vase in matte white, unmarked, 6" h, and spherical Leaves and Berries vase, unmarked, 6-1/2" h, **$60-$70** each.

Lizard vase, stoneware, 1930s, unmarked, 9" h, **$350-$450**.

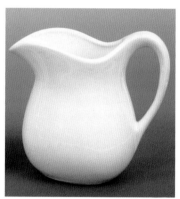

Pitcher vase, 1970s (later version of a 1940s piece), USA mark or unmarked, 5" h, **$25-$35**.

Large Swan vase and two-handled vase, both in gold trim, 1950s to 1960s, McCoy USA, 9" h, **$90-$100** each.

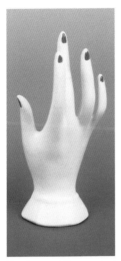

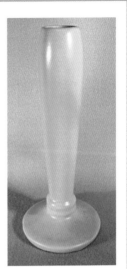

Hand vase with separated fingers and painted nails, 1950s, NM USA mark, 6-1/2" h, **$125-$150**.

Pitcher vase, 1950s, McCoy USA mark, 7-1/2" h, **$25-$35**.

Bud vase in matte yellow glaze, 1960s, McCoy mark, 8" h, **$35-$45**.

Two bud vases, cold painted, 1958, McCoy USA mark, and an indistinct style number, 6-1/2" h, **$45+** each.

Ram's Head vase in matte white (rare, usually chartreuse, black, or burgundy), 1950s, McCoy mark, 9-1/2" h, **$250-$300**; in other colors, **$100-$125**.

Four 5" basket-weave vases in glossy burgundy, green, white, and blue, **$40-$50** each.

Two versions of the Swan vase, white swan made in 1946, McCoy Made in USA mark; black swan made in 1953, 1950s McCoy mark, 9" h, **$65-$75** each.

Two Hand vases in matte aqua, 1940s, NM USA mark, 7-1/2" h, **$125-$150**; 5" h, **$55-$65**.

J.W. McCoy ewer vase in Carnelian glaze, left, and Rosewood grapes vase, early 1900s, both unmarked; ewer, 7-1/2" h, **$200-$225**; vase, 6-1/2" h, **$190-$250**.

J.W. McCoy vases with Carnelian glaze, early 1900s, marked 10, 8-1/4" h, **$200-$225**; 6-1/2" h, **$125-$150**.

Handled urn vase in Brown Onyx glaze with turquoise highlights, stoneware, 1930s, unmarked, 10" h, **$125+**.

Footed vase in Brown Onyx glaze, 1930s, unmarked, 12" h, **$90+.**

Tall fan vase in atypical glossy white (normally found in chartreuse and green, or yellow and maroon), mid-1950s, McCoy mark, 15" h, also found in 10"; as shown, **$350-$400**; same size, other colors, **$150-$200**; 10" size, **$75-$90**.

From left: Fin or Ribbed vase in matte white, 14" h, unmarked, **$250-$300**. Fin or Ribbed planter in matte white, 7" h, unmarked (may also be found with saucer base), **$90-$110**.

Fin floor vase in hard-to-find blue over blue-drip glaze, 1930s, stoneware, 14" h, unmarked, also came in a variety of matte glazes, **$250-$325**.

Floor vase in a Blue Onyx glaze, 24" h, unmarked, **$700-$900**.

Shrimp vase in traditional colors, 1950s, McCoy USA mark, 9" h, **$175+**.

Vase (collectors call this the "Shrimp vase" because of its common coloration) with applied maple leaves in atypical blue-black and yellow glaze (usually in chartreuse or salmon with green leaves), 1950s, McCoy USA mark, 9" h; as shown, **$600+**; in common colors, **$175-$225**.

Two vases in matte coral and aqua, the coral is smooth and aqua is faceted, 1940s, NM mark, 9" h, **$55-$65** each.

Two vases in glossy coral and yellow, 1950s, McCoy mark, 9" h, **$60-$70** each.

Glossy green vase with florist sticker, 1940s, no mark, these came in a variety of glazes both glossy and in a pastel matte finish, 8" h, **$55-$75**.

Vase in glossy yellow (rare, sometimes called an Arrow Leaf but different from other vases in that form), 1950s, McCoy mark, 8" h, **$550-$600**.

Typical 1940s pastel wheat vase, with hand-painted version on right, 1940s McCoy mark, 8-1/4" h; plain, **$40-$50**; hand painted, **$85-$110**.

Two vases in glossy white, late 1950s, unmarked, 8-1/2" and 8-1/4" h, vase at left has transfer decoration of roses, **$45-$55**; vase on right, **$65-$75**.

Vase in matte brown and green, 12" h, **$150-$175**.

Two matte white vases, one with leaves (Stoneware, late 1920s), one with loop handles, 1930s, unmarked, 12" h, **$200-$250**; 10" h, **$100-$125**.

From left: "V" vase in glossy green glaze, mid-1920s, V2 mark, this style also found without handles, 9" h, **$90-$110**. "Number 50" vase in glossy burgundy, 1930s, unmarked, 9" h, **$100-$125**.

Three 9" matte white vases, from left: two-handled vase, 1930s, McCoy mark; large Swan vase, 1950s, colored glazes were generally earlier, mid-1940s; Sailboat vase, seen here with round bottom, sailboat motif also found on narrower vase with square bottom, **$70-$90** each.

Vase with low drape handles in glossy blue glaze, 1940s, unmarked, 10" h, **$80-$90**.

Vase once thought to be Shawnee but later found in a McCoy catalog page, late 1940s, unmarked, 6-1/2" h, **$35-$45**.

Left: two-handled vase with post-factory decoration, 1940s, NM mark (reproductions found with McCoy mark), 9" h, **$40-$45**. Right: Lizard handle vase in matte white with post-factory decoration, mid- to late-1930s, unmarked, 9" h (also comes in 10"), **$200-$225**; this is also found in green and brown.

Two vases in gold trim, from left: Ivy motif (also called English Ivy), 1950s, McCoy USA mark, 9" h, **$150-$175**. Tulip motif, 1950s, USA mark, also with hand-applied inscription, "M.W. Rosendahl, 1955," 8" h, **$100-$125**.

Two vases in glossy yellow and pink with gold trim, 1950s, McCoy USA and Shafer marks, also found in blue and white, 9" h, **$90-$110** each.

Two presentation vases in gold trim, from left: Tulip motif, 1950s, McCoy mark, also with hand-applied inscription, "50 Golden Years" and signed E.P. Aurand, 8" h; McCoy mark, with hand-applied inscription, "1949 Iowa State Glad Show, Waterloo," signed E.P.A., 9" h, **$125-$150** each.

Two Disc vases in glossy cobalt blue and burgundy, 1940s, also found in yellow and white, USA mark, 6-3/4" h, **$100-$125** each.

Grape pitcher vase in matte white, 9" h, early 1950s, McCoy mark, **$50-$60**.

Three tall Cornucopia vases in matte white, 1930s, unmarked, 5" h, **$75-$100**; 8" h, **$50-$75**; 10" h, **$100-$125**.

Tall Scroll vase in matte green (often found in glossy tan-brown), late 1940s, USA mark, 14" h, **$150-$200**.

Non-production vase with carved leaves and branches, 1948, McCoy Made in USA mark with initials "TK," ex-Ty Kuhn collection, 8" h, no established value.

Two vases in matte aqua, 1940s, unmarked or USA mark, 9" h, **$50-$60** each.

Two vases in matte yellow and aqua, 1940s, NM USA mark, also found in white, 8" h, **$50-$60** each.

Two vases with leaves and stylized flowers in glossy green and matte aqua, stoneware, late 1920s, unmarked, 7" h, **$110-$125** each.

Left: vase in glossy aqua with hand-painted flowers, 1940s, McCoy mark, 8" h, **$125-$150** because of painting; normally, **$60-$70**. Right: Cornucopia vase in glossy aqua, 1940s, round McCoy mark, 7" h, **$50-$60**.

Left: Fluted vase with zigzag top in glossy aqua, 1950s, McCoy USA mark, 10" h (also found in 8" and 14" sizes), **$90-$110**. Right: vase in glossy aqua, 1940s, unmarked or NM mark, 8" h, **$50-$60**.

Two matte aqua vases, 9" and 7", from left: Swan vase, 1940s, McCoy mark, **$55-$65**; Cornucopia vase, 1940s, McCoy mark, **$45-$55**.

Two vases in glossy aqua, from left: 1940s, round McCoy mark, 9" h, **$45-$55**; Square Cherry vase, stoneware, 1930s, round McCoy mark, 12" h, **$125-$150**.

From left: two-handled vase in glossy aqua, 1940s, McCoy mark, **$50-$60**. Uncle Sam vase in glossy aqua, 1940s, incised McCoy mark, 7-1/2" h, also found in yellow and white, **$60-$70**. Beware of reproductions, which may be slightly smaller.

Floor vase in matte aqua, stoneware, 1930s or '40s, unmarked, matte and glossy colors, 18" h, **$1,200+** (rare at this size).

Three vases in glossy aqua, from left: 8" h, round McCoy USA mark, **$25-$35**; 12" h, McCoy USA mark, also found in yellow and white, **$50-$60;** 7-1/2" h, round McCoy USA mark, found in other colors, **$25-$35**.

Two vases, one with fired-on decoration (possibly a lunch-hour piece), 1940s, USA mark, 10" h; with decoration, **$125-$150**; without, **$75-$90**.

Vase with fired-on decoration, art nouveau influence similar to Brush-McCoy, 1920s, unmarked, 8" h, **$450-$500**.

Two matte aqua vases, 10" h, found in other matte colors, top: unmarked, **$85-$95**; bottom: arrow leaf, McCoy mark, **$125-$150**.

Left: Sailboat vase with square bottom in matte aqua, 1940s, NM USA or NM mark, other matte colors, 9" h, **$85-$95**. Right: two-handled vase in matte aqua, 1940s, McCoy mark, other matte colors, 9" h, **$55-$65**.

Two matte aqua vases, 10" and 11-1/2" h, from left: 1940s, USA mark, **$75-$85**; 1930s, unmarked, Stoneware, **$150-$175**; also found in sizes ranging from 6" to 18".

Two matte aqua vases, 9" h, from left: 1940s, McCoy mark, found in both matte and glossy colors, **$55-$65**; urn vase, 1940s, USA mark, rarely found in other matte colors, **$75-$85**.

Two matte aqua vases, 12" h, from left: 1940s, NM mark, frequently found with spots of other glazes, commonly cobalt blue, **$150-$175**; strap vase, usually found in glossy colors, **$175-$225**.

Two matte aqua floor vases, 14" h, from left: rib or fin vase, 1930s, unmarked, matte colors or drip glazes, **$500+**. Sand Dollar vase, 1930s and '40s, unmarked, matte or glossy colors, **$250-$300**.

Two matte aqua vases, 8" and 7", from left: Tulip vase, 1940s, USA mark, matte and glossy colors, **$75-$85**. Leafy vase, found in matte colors, 1940s, unmarked, **$150-$175**.

Two matte aqua vases, 8-1/2" and 10", from left: 1940s, round McCoy USA mark, found in matte and glossy colors, **$65-$75**; 1940s, McCoy mark, other matte colors, **$65-$75**.

A grouping of what collectors call the "5-inch vases," though actual sizes vary by up to half an inch. Many vase styles are hard to find this size, and so this has become an entire collecting category. They are unmarked. Prices vary from about **$60** to more than **$125** depending on style, glaze, and mold quality, and how badly a collector needs one to complete a set.

Wall Pockets

Wall pockets by nature are easily damaged, so collectors should look for signs of restoration around chipped holes and on high points, and paint touch-ups on those made with cold-paint decoration. Examples in gold trim command a higher price.

Apple wall pocket in gold trim, 1950s, unmarked, 7" l, **$200-$225**.

Bananas wall pocket, green leaves, with gold trim, 1950s, unmarked, 7" l, **$400-$450**.

Grapes wall pocket in gold trim, 1950s, unmarked, 7" l, **$300-$350**.

Bellows wall pocket, McCoy USA mark, 9" l, **$85+**.

Bird on sunflower wall pocket, can also stand as planter, McCoy mark, 6-3/4" h, **$50+**.

Clown or Jester wall pocket with cold-paint decoration, 1940s, McCoy mark, 8-1/2" l, **$90-$110**, depending on paint condition.

Blossomtime wall pocket in matte yellow, McCoy mark, 7-3/4" l, **$90-$110**.

Butterfly wall pocket in matte aqua with crisp mold, 1940s, NM mark, 6" h, **$450-$550**.

Cuckoo Clock wall pocket in gold trim (comes with both Roman and Arabic numerals, and in a range of colors), 1950s, McCoy mark, 8" h without weights, **$200-$225;** without gold trim, **$100-125**

Dutch shoe wall pocket with applied rose, 1950s, McCoy USA mark, 7-1/2" l, **$30+**.

Pair of Rustic glaze flower wall pockets, late 1940s, no mark, came in a variety of colors, 6" square, **$35-$45** each.

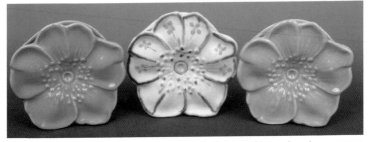

Three Flower form wall pockets, late 1940s, unmarked, 6" h; the blue and coral are common colors, **$40-$50**; the center pocket, with under-glaze decoration, is **$175-$225**.

Fan wall pocket with crisp mold, found in other colors and in gold trim, 1950s, McCoy USA mark, 8-1/2" w; **$75+**.

Fan wall pocket with crisp mold and unusual multi-color glaze, 1950s, McCoy USA mark, also signed by Nelson McCoy, 8-1/2" w; no other example with these variations is known, **$5,000+**.

Basket-weave Horn of Plenty wall pocket, 1950s, McCoy USA mark, 8" l, **$100-$120**.

Iron on a Trivet wall pocket, 1950s, McCoy USA, 8" l, **$85-$95**.

Lady in the Bonnet wall pocket with cold-paint decoration, 1940s, McCoy mark, wide variety of paint colors and details, 8" l, **$70-$80**.

Lily wall pocket in yellow, McCoy mark, 6-1/2" l, **$80-$100**.

Lovebirds on a Trivet wall pocket, 1950s, McCoy USA mark, 8" l, **$75-$85**.

Fancy Lily Bud wall pocket in matte aqua, 1940s, incised McCoy mark, 8" l, **$225-$250**.

Large Lily Bud wall pocket in matte aqua, 1940s, NM USA mark, 8" l, **$150-$175**.

Mailbox wall pocket, early 1950s, McCoy USA mark, also found with cold-paint decoration, **$90-$110**. Beware of reproductions in bright pastels.

Umbrella wall pocket, 1950s, McCoy USA mark, found in other colors including gold Brocade Line, 8-1/4" l, **$75-$85**.

Leaves and Berries wall pocket or smokeless ashtray, found in other colors, McCoy mark, 7" h, **$40+**.

Mexican Man wall pocket in matte aqua, 1940s, NM USA mark, 7-1/2" l, **$65-$75**.

Owls on a Trivet wall pocket with some cold-paint decoration, 1950s, McCoy USA mark, 8" l, **$75-$85**.

Urn wall pocket in speckled pink glaze with gold trim, McCoy USA mark, also found in chartreuse, 4-1/2" l, **$75-$85**.

Tongue wall pocket from the Floral Country line, 1970s, with decal decoration, 9-1/4" h, **$35+**.

Violin wall pocket in black, a hard to find color, **$350-$400**; in blue and gold, **$275-$325**

Miscellaneous

This section includes ashtrays, bookends, banks, console bowls, boxes, ornaments and other accessories, and some rare non-production pieces.

Ashtray, a lunch-hour piece, with applied heart and the words "MA" and "PA," marked McCoy on reverse, made from the bottom of a Cornucopia vase, 6-1/2" x 3-1/4", no established value.

Sailor with sack bank, Seaman's Bank for Savings, 1950s, 5-1/2" h, **$45+**.

Mercury Friendship 7 ashtray/bank, unmarked, 4-3/4" h, **$45+**.

Kittens and barrel bank, 1975, Lancaster Colony mark, 6-1/2", **$100+**.

Covered bridge bank, 1975, Lancaster Colony mark, 6" h, **$100+**.

Brooklyn Savings Bank, 1960s, 6" l, **$60+**.

Williamsburg Savings Bank with pen holder, 1960s, also marked "Tower of Strength – Central Office Tower," 7-1/2" h, **$40+**.

Mile marker bank, marked "This mile marker made exclusively for the friends of First Federal Savings and Loan – Zanesville, Ohio," 8" h, **$25+**.

Beer barrel bank, 1960s, cold painted, marked "Metz Premium Beer," and "Metz Brewing Company - Omaha, Nebraska," 6-1/4" h, **$50+**.

Schlitz small tankard and tankard-form bank, 1960s, 5-3/4" and 7-3/4" h, bank with cork stopper; tankard, **$20+**; bank, **$45+**.

Smiley face bank, with worn cold paint, 1970s, 6-1/4" diameter, **$35+**.

Piggy bank with cold-painted corn and unpainted pig planter, 1950s, each 5-1/2" l, bank with raised McCoy mark, planter unmarked; bank, **$40+**; planter, **$20+**.

Eagle bank, 1960s, marked "The National Bank of Dayton," 8" h, **$50+**.

Two owl banks, 1960s, one marked "Western Savings Bank," one marked "Manhattan Savings bank," found with other markings, each 7-1/2" h, **$45+** each.

Basketball bank, with gold trim, 1960s, hand lettered "Lancaster Hi," 4-3/4" diameter, **$75+**.

Zanesville, Ohio, bicentennial commemorative bank, Century National Bank, 1997, Nelson and Billie McCoy – The McCoy Collection mark, also signed by Nelson and Billie McCoy, numbered 1912 out of 1997, 6" h, **$45+**.

Ohio Bicentennial bank, 1803-2003, Made in Ohio – The McCoy Collection mark, also signed by Nelson McCoy, 6-1/4" h, **$50+**.

First Ohio Statehouse bank, 2003, McCoy Collection 2003 Made in Ohio mark, 6-1/2" h, 5-1/2" square, **$50+**.

Football bank, with gold trim, 1960s, with decal, "Mississippi State University 1878," found with other school markings, 6-3/4" l, **$75+**.

Teddy Bear bank, McCoy 1848-1998 Sesquicentennial, with scarf and medallion, McCoy Collection mark, also signed by Nelson and Billie McCoy, numbered 738 out of 1500, 7" h, **$45+**.

Bookend planters in brown and tan, unusual this color combination, 1950s, McCoy USA mark, 6-1/2" h, **$150+**.

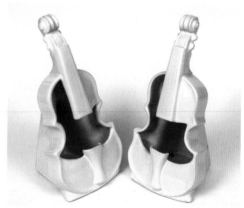

Bass-fiddle bookend planters, 1960s, McCoy USA, 9-3/4" h, **$125+**.

From left: Hungover dog bank made for Swank, 1960s, unmarked, 6" h; Eagle bank, 1960s, unmarked, 7" h, **$50-$60** each.

Rearing-horse bookends, with gold trim, 1970s, USA mark, 8" h, **$125+** with gold trim.

Lily bookends with pearly glaze in gold trim, 1940s to '50s, sometimes marked McCoy USA, usually unmarked, 5-1/2" h, **$225-$275**/pair; other colors, **$125-$150**/pair.

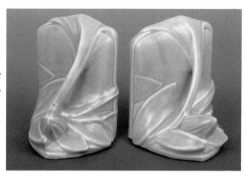

Lily Bud bookends in matte aqua, 1940s, NM USA mark, 5-3/4" h, **$200-$250**/pair.

Parakeets (also called lovebirds) bookends in matte aqua, early 1940s, NM mark, **$200-$250**/pair.

Centerpiece bowl with candleholders in matte green, 1930s, stoneware, unmarked, bowl 8-1/2" diameter, candleholders 5" diameter, also came in the brown and green matte finish, **$150-$200** set.

Swallow bookends/planter, 1950s, McCoy USA mark, 6" h, **$275-$325**/pair.

Lily Bud console bowls in 5-1/2" and 11-1/2" widths, 1940s, NM mark; 5-1/2", **$40-$50**; 11-1/2", **$125-$150**. Two Lily Bud candleholders in matte aqua, 1940s, NM mark, 5-1/2" diameter, **$75-$85**/pair.

Console bowl with grapes in traditional colors, 1950s, McCoy USA mark, 10-1/4" w, **$60+**.

Cuspidor with grapes motif in glossy brown, 1940s, unmarked, 7-1/2" diameter, **$50-$60**.

Console bowl with candleholders, stoneware, late 1930s, more common in green, bowl 8" diameter, **$350-$450**/set; in green, **$200**/set.

Double candleholder, 1930s (?), raised McCoy mark but not a production piece, 9-1/2" h, only two others known to exist in the Cope Gallery, no established value.

Pink and blue stoneware hurricane lamp candleholders, 1970s, unmarked, base 4-1/2" h, with shade 13-1/2", **$40-$50** /pair.

Hands novelty dish (sometimes called an ashtray) in gold trim, 1940s, NM USA mark, 5-3/4" l, **$70-$80**.

Three-section Leaf candy or snack dish, early 1950s, McCoy mark, 11" wide, also found in Rustic glazes of green and brown. As shown, **$100-$125**; Rustic, **$50-$60**.

Lid from a covered casserole in the form of a long-billed bird with crest, lid also found in glossy brown but without crest, no established value.

Freddie the grass-growing Gleep, 1960s, glazed top and bottom, 8-1/2" h, **$45+**.

Butterfly Line console dish or platter, 1940s, NM USA mark, found in other matte colors, 14" long, **$350-$400**.

Pickling crock and butter churn, with original tag and dasher, Lancaster Colony, 1980s, 12-1/2" h, **$60-$70** each.

Non-production nut dish in leaves motif, McCoy mark, only a dozen known to exist, **$300-$350**.

Apollo LM decanter prototype (?), 1969, with cork stopper, unmarked, not a production style, 7-1/2" h, no established value.

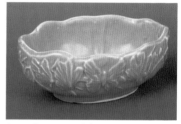

Butterfly Line pin dish (also called console bowl) in matte blue and yellow, 1940s, NM USA mark, 5" diameter, **$55-$65**.

Two Cinnamon Bears, one a refrigerator deodorizer, the other a bank, with fiber ties holding a cinnamon stick and a penny, limited to 500 each, McCoy Limited USA mark, also signed by Nelson and Billie McCoy, each 5" h, **$60+** /pair.

Two Brocade pieces: round covered dish and trinket box, possibly part of a dresser set, 1950s, McCoy USA 464 mark, **$80-$90**/pair.

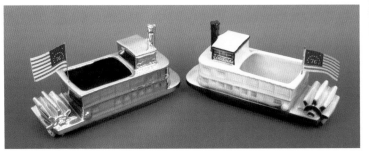

Commemorative steamboats (the "Lorena") made for Zanesville Chamber of Commerce, 1976, 7" long; **$70-$80** each.

Apollo decanter with nose cone, 1969, cork stopper, marked "Thomas W. Sims Distillery - Stanley KY USA – Dec. 1968-69" and impressed logo, 10-1/2" h, **$50+**.

Apollo astronaut decanter, 1970, cork stopper, marked "Thomas W. Sims Distillery - Stanley KY – 203 – Dec. 1968 July 1969," 11" h, **$95+**.

Golf-motif decanter, impressed artist name, M.A. Bucci, marked on the bottom, "Nelson and Billie McCoy, The McCoy Collection – Zanesville, Ohio - 1997 – GSMC Pro-Am," for Good Samaritan Medical Center, 8-1/2" h, **$65**.

Double Angelfish and Seahorses flower bowl ornaments or aquarium decorations, 1940s, unmarked, 6" and 6-1/4" h, also found in green. Fish, **$200-$250**; Seahorses, **$300-$350**.

1932 Pierce Arrow decanter made for Jim Beam, 1960s, McCoy mark, 11" l, **$75-$85**.

Jupiter 60 train decanter set, made for McCormick Whiskey, Mt. Clemens MCP mark, 1969, produced to commemorate the 100th anniversary of the driving of the golden spike near Promontory, Utah; includes locomotive (12" long), wood tender, mail car and passenger car, **$250-$350**.

Racehorse dresser caddie made for Swank with clothes brush tail, 1960s, unmarked, 9" l not including tail, **$75-$85**.

Bull dresser caddie made for Swank, 1960s, unmarked, 10" l, **$25-$35**.

Dog dresser caddie made for Swank with shoehorn tail, 1960s, unmarked, 11" l, **$45-$55**.

Cuervo Tequila set with platter, two cups and salt bowl, 1970s, 8-3/4" w, cups 1-3/4" h, **$100+**.

From left: Fawn flower bowl ornament, (one of the "ladder pieces," so named because they were pictured in an early McCoy guide on a drying rack that was tiered like the steps of a ladder), 1940s to 1950s, usually found in white or brown glaze, this one is ex-Ty Kuhn collection and painted by Kuhn; as shown, **$175-$200**; normally, **$90-$110**. Goat planter, 1950s, McCoy USA mark, **$300-$350**.

Lion statue, 1960s, unmarked, 15" l, **$45-$55**.

Three flower bowl ornaments or flower holders (fish), 1940s-1950s, usually found in white, yellow, green, or brown glaze, USA or unmarked; fish, 3" h, **$150-$200**; rabbit, 1-1/2" h, **$300-$350**.

Four flower bowl ornaments (the witch, gnome, and pelican are "ladder pieces," so named because they were pictured in an early McCoy guide on a drying rack that was tiered like the steps of a ladder), 1940s-1950s, usually found in white or brown (rare) glaze, USA or unmarked, about 3" h; cat and witch, **$400-$450**; gnome, **$300-$325**; pelican, **$400-$425**.

Fish flower bowl ornament (one of a kind?), 1950s, USA mark, 4-1/2" h, **$2,300+**.

"First Flight" figurine, 2002, signed by Nelson and Billie McCoy, inscribed 5502, made by Buckeye Stoneware, 11-1/2" h, **$40+**.

Mini jug in deep forest green, 1960s, unmarked, **$20-$25**.

Inhaler replica, 9" h, **$30-$35**.

Five flower bowl ornaments in matte white (the first four from left are "ladder pieces," so named because they were pictured in an early McCoy guide on a drying rack that was tiered like the steps of a ladder), 1940s, usually found in white or brown (rare) glaze, unmarked, from 3-3/4" to 4-3/4" h, **$100-$125** each.

Items made for Schering Pharmaceutical Co., from left: Coricidin Cosmas & Damian mortar with wooden pestle, 5" h, marked Schering on bottom. Galen mug, 3-1/2" h, marked Schering; mortar/ pestle, **$25-$30**; mug, **$10-$15**.

From left: Nelson and Billie McCoy retirement mug, 1981, **$100-$125**; Nelson McCoy Pottery Co. mug, **$80-$90**.

Turtle sprinkler, with original label and cold-painted details, 1950s, McCoy USA mark, 9-1/2" l, **$65+**.

Football paperweight, marked "Roseville Jr. High 1971," worn, and "Kevin Williams" on reverse, 3-3/4" l, **$75+**.

Trinket box in atypical glaze, 1970s, McCoy USA mark, ex-Ty Kuhn collection, **$90-$110**.

American eagle wall plaque, two mounting holes, unmarked, 15" w, 4-1/4" h, **$55+**.

More Essential Insight and Illustration

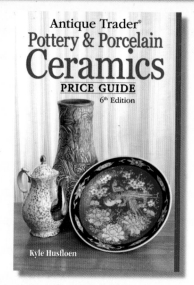

Antique Trader® Pottery & Porcelain Ceramics Price Guide
6th Edition
by Kyle Husfloen

Identifying and assessing pottery and porcelain is never more easy or accurate than when you have this guide in hand. This guide delivers detailed coverage of American, English, European and Oriental ceramics produced between the 18th and mid-20th century, with makers' mark facts, and up-to-date collector pricing represented in the 10,000 listings.

Now in full-color, this all-inclusive reference supports your identifying efforts with its wide variety of collectible ceramics in the more than 3,500 photos included. Whether you are fascinated by Grueby and Lotus Ware, or are a long-time fan of Hadley or Red Wing, you won't be without something to admire in this go-to guide.

Softcover • 6 x 9 • 768 pages
100 b&w photos • 3,500 color photos
Item# Z3648 • $25.99